A Meeting of Mystic Paths

Christianity and Yoga

A MEETING OF MYSTIC PATHS

CHRISTIANITY AND YOGA

JUSTIN O'BRIEN

Yes International Publishers
St. Paul, Minnesota

YES International Publishers
1317 Summit Avenue, St. Paul, MN 55105-2602
612-645-6808

Library of Congress Cataloging-in-Publication Data

O'Brien, Justin.
    A meeting of mystic paths : Christianity and yoga / Justin
O'Brien.
        p.   cm.
    Includes bibliographical references and index.
    ISBN 0-936663-14-6
    1. Christianity and yoga.   I. Title.
BR128. Y630265   1966
261.2' 45--dc20   96-14872
                                                        CIP

Printed in the United States of America

CONTENTS

FOREWORD

Several years ago Swami Rama of the Himalayas remarked to me, "One of the beautiful gems of Christian tradition is found in the words of Jesus where he said, 'No one comes to the Father but by me' (John 14:6). Unfortunately," he continued, "it appears that possibly half of Christendom takes this to mean that anyone who isn't baptized and a practicing Christian is excluded from communion with God, while it seems about as many more speak apologetically as if either Jesus had been misreported or made an audacious claim he had no business making. But we see that his claim was to Christ Consciousness or consciousness of the true Self which is divine. Jesus Christ had every right to say what he is reported to have said. And while our terminology may differ, we also say, there is no other way to God."

I concurred. Yet thinking back over my life, especially to the years spent in training and preparation for the vocation and ministry of an Episcopal priest, I recalled the time when Swami Rama's sage observation and witness, at the very least, would have caught me by surprise. Surely my paramount question would have been, How could one who practices a spirituality which isn't even regarded as religion, let alone Christian religion, seriously make such a Christian affirmation? Would I have welcomed the state of puzzlement into which he would have thrown me? The counsel of Jesus to his disciples might have come to my aid: "Whoever is not against us is for us" (Luke 9:50; Mark 9:40). My youthful zeal to disavow any claim to truth which sounded as if it hadn't derived from the Bible might likewise have been dealt a healthy blow by the magnanimous insight of the apostle John: "Whoever is a loving person has been born of God and knows God" (1 John 4:7).

So I mused and mused again. Could I, likewise, twenty-five years ago, have appreciated as readily and thankfully as I do today the offering presented in Dr. Justin O'Brien's splendid book, *A Meeting of Mystic Paths: Christianity and Yoga?* Would the sound of the book's title alone have struck me as suspect?

You, no doubt, have pondered its title, read its table of contents and allowed its cover to register in your mind. Now you may wonder whether or not you're really looking for what it may have to offer. Or, perhaps, with more or less than I of living, searching, wrestling and practicing on the spiritual journey, already you have come to anticipate the important contribution this work may prove itself to be. Either way, I believe, a wealth of insight awaits you as you read.

Jesus taught, "Behold the Kingdom of God is within you...like a treasure hidden in a field!" (Luke 17:21; Matthew 13:44). Socrates, in Plato's *Phaedrus* says, "I must first know myself, as the Delphinian inscription says. To be curious about that which is not my concern, while I am still in ignorance of my own self, would be ridiculous." Dr. O'Brien has long taken such counsels to heart and made of them a living practice. Perhaps you also glory in the name Christian but are of the inclusive and not the exclusive kind. If so, you meet in Justin O'Brien a strong companion in the Way. He is richly qualified to write with authority about yoga and Christianity–about the converging paths. Here a rich fare awaits the reader. Let us speak a word of blessing and savor the feast!

Ralph C. Roth, M. Div.
Trinity Church
Mount Pocono, Pennsylvania

FOREWORD

This book builds bridges between the tradition of Christianity and the science of yoga. The word yoga is much misunderstood in the Western hemisphere; some see yoga as a fad and others as a kind of religion. Actually yoga is a systematic science, a set of techniques, and while yoga itself is not a religion, its practical teachings are an integral part of the great religions of the world. The Book of Genesis, the Sermon on the Mount, and the Book of Revelations all contain yogic teachings, and in the Psalms there are numerous references to the yogic method of meditation.

The origins of yoga are obscure and go back many thousands of years. Its central teaching is that our essential nature is divine, perfect, and infinite. We remain unaware of this reality, however, because we constantly identify with our bodies, minds, and external objects. That false identification makes us think and feel that we are imperfect and limited, subject to sorrow, death, and decay. Comparing the science of yoga with the great religions of the world, particularly Christianity, one realizes that yoga science offers practical methods to aspirants of any religion, so that they can know the center of consciousness within. Through the meditative methods of yoga one can dispel the darkness of ignorance, and become aware of our essential nature, which is free from all imperfections.

The author of this book, Dr. Justin O'Brien, is eminently qualified to write about both the yogic tradition and Christianity. He has been a respected teacher of philosophy and theology for thirty years, and a serious student of yoga for over twenty-five years. His work creates a bridge to greater understanding on the part of Westerners for the practical utility of the yogic techniques so that they can enhance the spiritual growth and transformation of Christians and deepen their own rich tradition.

Swami Rama
Rishikesh, Himalayas

PREFACE

The breadth of diversity in Christian spirituality startles even Christians. A careful examination of Christianity over the centuries demonstrates that Christian spirituality is not a single thread any more than Christian faith is one exclusive denomination. Spirituality is like a tapestry requiring many dyed threads woven together to form a masterpiece.

Likewise, those rituals and ceremonies that play an important part in the Christian churches have a long, ennobling history influenced by many diverse elements. For example, the Catholic Mass, like the Jewish Seder, features a sacred meal, which itself is common to many ancient religious rites. The use of incense, candles, food, fire, bodily gestures, and special garments in Christian liturgical occasions, although varied in style, trace their origin to ancient Eastern ritual. The underlying unity in these items is their appreciation as sacred things, that is, something sacramental. Among the sacred things of the world, Christians accord precedence to human beings, for they are the image and likeness of God.

Knowledge of the complexities of human nature is not the prerogative of one science any more than Christian values belong exclusively to one church. This human nature that bears a sacred imprint displays a versatility expressed over the centuries in many cultures. History is one long drama depicting how peoples acknowledge or resent their nature and destiny.

In my travels in the East and West I have been fortunate to meet and experience some of today's episodes in this ongoing drama. What caught my interest were the recurring questions that citizens of many countries raised about the benefits and deficiencies that they sensed in their customary forms and practices of spirituality. There were many who doubted and resented the Christian influences of their upbringing. There were those who sensed that Christian values are richer than their best presentation by an institutional church. There were those who suspected that Christianity may have benefits yet to be discovered by the search for the meaning of life.

From exposure to these questionings over the years, this book took shape. To all these attitudes I have attempted to bring a rich tradition from the Himalayas. The science of yoga displays a perspective on human nature that may astonish in its optimism. By contrasting and comparing both traditions, I hope to provoke readers to look at Christianity from a new perspective and encourage dialog from a sense of the truth of both. In this reflection and experimentation, modern seekers can thus be aided in their quest for spiritual fulfillment.

JOB

TRADITIONS IN TANDEM

In the second century, St. Justin Martyr said, "Whatever has been nobly spoken in any place is a part of Christian heritage."[1] The winds of history blow a new climate in today's Christianity as it carries forward the words of the past. In these final years of the twentieth century, traditional Western approaches to religious thought and spirituality are undergoing revision. We are recognizing those nobly spoken words from many places that have long inspired fellow seekers. We are learning that genuine spirituality exists in many guises. We are admitting that pluralism in approaches does not endanger one's preferred beliefs nor reduce traditions to meaningless equality. Rather these times are, as St. Justin advised, expanding the Christian heritage.

The Vatican's recognition of the importance of other traditions was proclaimed by Archbishop Jean Jadot:

> ...we are now far more vividly aware that several religious traditions such as the Hindu and the Buddhist and the Chinese traditions point to rich fonts of spirituality which they describe as 'sacred or holy literature,' their 'holy books.'...If such writings are part of mankind's spiritual heritage, should we not learn how to read them intelligently?

Could they not be a help for us to gain new insights and deepen our appreciation of our own Christian traditions? [2]

These statements characterize the new wind affecting mutual consideration among traditions. People are less fearsome in noticing truth preserved in other traditions. Similarly, the scientific comprehension of human nature, notably in the area of mind/body medicine, has undergone drastic revisions. Few medical schools, for example, would teach that human volition cannot affect the autonomic nervous system. On the contrary, experimental evidence has thoroughly demonstrated that the human mind can duly influence any region of the body.[3] While these ideas seem new in our culture, the broad acknowledgment of mind over matter has always been a basic tenet of the ancient science of yoga.

An understanding of human nature is essential to spiritual growth and transformation. Theologically speaking, it is a common principle that creation is a revelation to mankind of the meaning of God. Since in the Hebrew Torah, Genesis singles out men and women as the image and likeness of divinity, it would be reasonable to expect that the more one knows about human nature, individually and collectively, the more one could fathom the ultimate source of reality.

To this extent, yoga, while not a religion, presents to followers of any religion an opportunity for systematic growth in self-knowledge. Yoga belongs to the wisdom heritage of humankind, brought to us by the early Himalayan sages. Its purpose is not merely physical health, suppleness, and peace of mind, though these are among the numerous benefits of yoga practices. Yoga's goal is to aid people in understanding themselves as completely as possible. Yoga does not pretend to supply cultural answers to modern-day problems but shows people how to deal with themselves in terms of discovering and actualizing their native endowment. Christians would, no doubt, appreciate a tradition that improves one's well-being and encourages the enrichment of their society.

Since yoga traces its many branches to the tradition of perennial wisdom, it is not surprising that some of its insight into human nature has been incorporated into religions and cultures over the centuries. Many of the hygienic practices for sound health that are a part of the contemporary scene, for example, are found in yoga manuals composed centuries ago. Likewise, some of the key ideas of yoga about physical, emotional, and mental balance now becoming familiar in the West are discernible in many walks of life. The Feldenkrais movements are rooted in hatha yoga, Neuro-Linguistic Programming principles are discernible in tantra yoga, Psychosynthesis incorporated much from yoga psychology—to name only a few enterprises that, while not always acknowledging their debt, nevertheless draw from the Himalayan yoga wisdom tradition.

THE PATH OF WORSHIP

When Christians gather together for religious services they are performing worship. In examining the more than 400 versions of Christianity in the Western hemisphere, it is evident that few of them dispense with worship. Christians, however, need to be reminded that liturgy is not unique to Christianity but is a universal action performed in ancient as well as modern times. Worship was obviously neither invented by Western religions nor is it only effective within Christian context.

Worship, or *puja* as it is called in the ancient *Vedas*—those venerable writings from the Himalayan sages—has always been viewed as a form for achieving the most profound union with the divine. Still continued today, the ancient ceremonies are carefully arranged so that their symbols convey to the participants the meaning of the life transformation taking place. In contrast, some Christians would narrow their acts of worship to a compulsion based on fear as if they were approaching a stern God who demands weekly compulsory attendance. Their action is less a joyful celebration than that of a debtor paying his just dues for fear of punitive damages. A reading of the words of Christ at the last supper within the context of John's Gospel reveals a very different interpretation. Here the meaning of worship approaches a recognition of participation in an uplifting, communal action that leads to human liberation. Worship becomes an inviting way to immortality, since those in community are joined with the divine through special acts.

Without knowing it, Christians, in their highest acts of worship, are akin to the practitioners of an ancient form of yoga, *bhakti* yoga. This is not a thin label pointing to surface similarities. The Sanskrit word is derived from a root word *bhava*, which means "from the heart." Genuine worship is more than paying a debt or uttering prayers; it is a heartfelt action that aims at banishing the distance of mundane living from the divine presence by rejoining one's existence to its life-giving origin. Christian liturgy functions in similar fashion as *bhakti* yoga; it is a way of offering oneself totally to the divine and signifying that commitment through devotion and reverence.

In worship one unites oneself reverentially to God. The worshipping community joins together to become enjoined to the divine. The visible act of joining to the divine life as it is enacted in various Christian churches unfolds throughout the ceremony and is especially signified at the time of communion. With this orientation, the burden of the community is to compose and enact liturgical services that truly express their devotion to their divine origin, enliven their gathering into a community of believers, and celebrate the richness of life.

Through the symbolism of the human acts of worship the universe returns itself in awareness to its divine origin for renewal. This is the meaning of sacrifice—from the Latin *sacra*, "sacred," and *ficere*, "to make"—to make holy. The notion of sacrifice is only incidentally related with killing. To sacrifice signifies transformation, moving from the mundane domain to the divine domain. In this way worship reminds people that they are more than the humdrum of life (what yoga refers to as *samsara* or "the wheel of life"), that they can engage a ritual signifying their true destiny. In celebrating existence, believers cast the humdrum into a different light by coming into loving contact with the source of existence. This devotional joining of human with the divine unites and restores, thus illustrating the meaning of *bhakti* yoga, "to yoke or unite with love." In this way, the Christian liturgy expresses a basic, universal aspiration in its followers and joins a wide range of traditions which have recognized the need for eternal life.

In addition, the expression of devotional love occurs in daily life, outside the context of formal worship. Individuals of all religions are drawn to use love as characteristic of their life. At the very heart of Christianity is the notion of love. To work and love others with the kind of breath and strength demonstrated by its founder becomes the impelling inspiration for his followers. In acknowledging this inspiration, Christians speak of doing actions in charitable service. This unselfish emphasis can focus the emotional power of love to base its practical expressions solely upon love of God. For some, the unconditional love of God becomes a dominant way of life, a spirituality, central to their thoughts and behaviors. The same aspiration is found in *bhakti* yoga where one can consolidate one's entire life. In the 8th-century Vedic philosopher Shankara's *Saundaryalahari*, "Through the act of self-surrender, let my prattle become recitation of your name, the movement of my limbs gestures of worship, my walk perambulation around you, my food sacrificial offering to you, my lying down prostration to you; whatever I do for my joy, let it become transformed into an act of worship to you."

Ultimately, life alone will beckon love's search. As lovers proceed on their path, they will be spontaneously challenged to expand their power of compassion to encompass life itself. They are moving out into a greater humanitarian concern for all that their lover has created. The rituals, the various objects and subjects that have been the fond direction for one's love, will be subsumed into a universal expansion that will love beyond the limitations of ceremony, caste, or any cultural priority until it embraces fully the inner union with the ultimate reality.

THE PATH OF ACTION

Many Christians are involved in professional and domestic actions that fulfill their talents as well as pay the bills. Both the intention and the consequent actions are directed towards the benefit of those who receive the action. In every community one can recognize people who are especially noted for being reliable, honest, and competent in their jobs. Equally important, one expects to find these same characteristics demonstrated by parents in their loving concern for their children. In these activities Christians would be practicing a form of yoga called *karma-marga*—the path of skillful actions.

Karma means action. No one can live without performing deeds. Hence the word *karma* is a Sanskrit designation for the inevitability of human actions and their consequences.

Those who expend themselves unselfishly for others, who recognize the value of excellence in their professional relations, who tactfully interact with peers, and who foster friendships with others are developing spiritually through the practice of these skillful actions. In *karma* yoga one speaks of doing these actions unselfishly, ensuring that the fruits or results reach the intended goal. In Christian circles, one speaks of developing virtues, especially the moral virtues that apply to everyday actions. When prudent decisions and a sense of justice guide one's actions towards others, then we have a demonstration of moral or skillful performance. The performance of one's duty skillfully—doing the right action at the right time—shapes human action, the *karma*, into moral virtue. Virtue means power. The proper expression of power not only results in the intended action but returns to the doer of the action as a strengthening of that same power. Skills are developed only in action. However, a caution arises. In business as in personal relations, one can become overly impressed with the importance of one's actions to the point where adhering to them blights the task. Often the issue is not the action itself but a growing attitude toward it. As I get emotionally associated with the task, I exaggerate my importance and thus associate its success or failure with my personal status. This gradual loss of objectivity dims, as yogis would say, the power of *vairagya*, the ability to keep one's inner attitude in disinterested balance.

Both Christianity and yoga offer the same challenging remedy to counteract that weakness. Christianity proposes that one work in a loving, just manner, even from a charitable motive. Yoga proposes that one does one's duties unselfishly. Both traditions stipulate that freedom from selfishness and stress lies in performing one's deeds from an abiding attitude of loving service. In this way, the strains of pettiness, self-aggrandizement, and greed for dominance are banished by higher aspirations. Here again these traditions uphold the human attitude of loving service for others which is universally recognized as a hallmark on the path to full spiritual maturity.

The Path of Knowledge

Tillich, Rahner, Zaehner, Lossky, James, Hocking, Marechal, Lonergan and many other theologians depict individuals who sought to grasp the intelligibility of the absolute. Their efforts were similar to those yogic sages over the centuries who practiced *jnana* yoga. Like the Church Fathers and medieval philosophers/theologians, these modern writers expressed their pursuit of the absolute under the inspiration of truth. Whereas devotion and service have characterized the first two examples of the Christian convergence with yoga, this path of human development reveals the conscious effort to understand the ultimate—first as a concept then as a reality. The pursuit of truth has led scientists, artists, writers and philosophers from the East and the West on an adventure in knowledge where gradually they have learned to discern reality from appearance. The yogic sages, like Christian mystics such as Meister Eckart, utilized the discriminatory power of the intellect, the *buddhi*, as a vehicle to uncover the mysteries of truth. For these adepts, the study of philosophy became a spiritual practice that led to enlightenment, to the possession of divine wisdom.

The power of the mind has the ability to live from the truth that one has experienced. *Jnana* yoga proposes that the love for truth can become the basis for a way of life that has enthralled men and women from every age. Serious Christians desire to know themselves, thus echoing an aspiration that is earlier than the writing of the Bible. Self-knowledge is a profound necessity, for without it one can barely hope to fathom the practicalities of life, let alone its ultimate meaning.

Hardly anyone would refuse wisdom. Yet only some Christians have labored on behalf of wisdom. Few aspirants would commit themselves to a philosophy that unflinchingly reaches beyond the intellect. Divine wisdom, however, is a knowledge which exceeds rational concepts.

Genuine philosophers, theologians and scientists are never satisfied with merely an intellectual familiarity with the world. They are induced by the contemplation of truth to exceed the senses and rational mind, to break through conventional paradigms. Thus they move from ordinary science (*apara vidya*) to the science of the absolute (*para vidya*). At this level of awareness, one experiences truth directly. Those who would practice *jnana* yoga are assisted with the writings of the *Upanishads* and Vedanta philosophy in which the study of *atma bodha*—the study of the self—receives priority. In contemplating the *Upanishads*, the aspirant encounters the twelve major spiritual treatises that constitute the richly mythological and philosophical portions of the *Vedas*. These writings were further reflected into a metaphysical system of philosophy called Vedanta. The goal is not unlike that of Christian philosophy: *samahitam*, a state of consciousness wherein all questions are resolved and one lives from the vision of divine wisdom. In studying the lives of the those Christians who tread the path of wisdom, we find that faith acted as a spur to the intellect to seek the direct experience of the absolute as far as human capacities can achieve it. Hence the compatibility of the Christian allegiance to the pursuit of highest truth with the path of *jnana* yoga, the way of immortal wisdom.

THE ROYAL PATH

While Christian mystics seem a strange lot and legends describe their lives as a series of incredible adventures, they are actually the most balanced of people, for they have involved their entire being in the pursuit of total fulfillment. Some of them have bequeathed to us their insights into the complexities of living in the world and keeping an eye on transcendent goals. Similar in approach is the broad path of *astanga* yoga, known more popularly as *raja* yoga—the royal route. This path is for someone who enjoys a holistic approach involving body, mind, and spirit. The famous eight rungs or stages in *raja* yoga comprise an overall development of the individual personality living an active life in society. It is an integrated path combining theory with practice, a way to fuse an inner life with engagement in the world.

In reading the works of St. John of the Cross, one finds an acute analysis of the mind, its faculties and its relationship to the body. The saint explains the adventure in higher consciousness by elaborating in detail the various movements, desires, imaginings and subconscious episodes that occur in spiritual growth. John shows that the spiritual undertaking has a rationale that, while not abstract nor stifling to the spirit, nevertheless reveals a definite causal order in spiritual growth. His contemporary, St. Teresa of Avila, describes in her journals the stages of human maturity toward spirituality with all its pitfalls in a manner that reminds the reader that this shrewd woman lived a full life of dealing with business decisions, setting up religious training centers, ceaseless travel, ecclesiastical politics, narrow censorship, and a host of resistances that could not appreciate her vision of life.

Likewise the major work of yoga, Patanjali's *Yoga Sutras*, reveals a map of consciousness that surprisingly concurs in many instances with both John's and Teresa's program for spiritual realization. Both authors describe the human ascent from the gross, sensual level to the subtlest, transcendental experiences that supersede rational awareness. Incorporated into the *Sutras* are the traditional threefold phases of purgation, illumination, and union that are described in many Christian manuals on spiritual development. The principal activity that centers the lives of Christian mystics as well as *raja* yogis is meditation. More than any other exercise, both traditions look to meditation as the *sine qua non* for spiritual evolution. From the obvious yoga disciplines of the Desert Fathers to the renaissance of meditation today, the Christian endorsement of meditation has a long and consistent history.

Then why do yoga and meditation seem to have come from the East and appear as something new for Christians? We live amidst cultural pressures and issues that clamor for attention. Sometimes the problems in society focus upon only certain aspects of a broad tradition. While every Christian tries to be charitable in daily life, for example, it was not until this century that many Christians saw the incompatibility of treating some human beings as slaves. Only recently have theologians pointed out how some church pronouncements have distorted the gospels to make women suffer in patronizing subservience to men. History shows that each generation retains the wisdom it chooses and later realizes what it overlooked. The tradition of meditation became, after the sixteenth century, an exclusive specialty for monks and nuns and so mingled with prayer that it lost its autonomy. The resurgence of interest in meditation among Christians today is a return to the crossroads where yoga and Christianity meet for the task of human perfection.

CONCLUSION

These paths of yoga—*bhakti, karma, jnana and raja*—are some of the various approaches that yoga science has developed for enabling people to understand the vast possibilities of living a joyful existence. Through careful comparisons of Christianity and yoga, one can recognize that the philosophy and practice of yoga will assist Christians to greater creativity as well as to a deeper understanding of the human spirit and the riches of their religious traditions.

THE WAYS OF RELIGIOUS CONSCIOUSNESS

Before beginning the story, let me set the stage. From out of the dynamism of their lives, people raise questions that have more than temporary significance to satisfy immediate survival or career needs. From this broader horizon, individuals desire to explain themselves, to arrive at a self-understanding that makes longevity more than tolerable, to view life as a totality that renders an ultimate meaning to their existence. It is from this unrestricted desire for ultimate meaning that human beings, individually as well as collectively, form what may be called their religious consciousness. And in most quarters of this planet throughout history, a special attitude of reverential awe accompanies the content of one's religious consciousness.

A STORY

Once upon a time there was a village situated in a valley near the Andes Mountains. The inhabitants had lived in this valley for many generations and grew to revere the awesome mountains with their snow peaks reaching into the heavens. On special days of the year the elders revealed to the people the sacredness of the mountains: it was these lofty peaks that brought the rainfall for the crops and protected them from all dangers. Seeing these distant peaks and remembering the consoling words, the villagers enjoyed a sense of profound security. They showed their reverence to the mountains by bowing to them upon rising from sleep and before retiring at night.

One day some young people decided that they wanted to walk out of the valley and investigate the mountains at close range. They announced this to their astonished parents who immediately ran to the elders for advice. The elders were also shocked at the proposal. No one in their history had ever considered climbing the mountains! They sternly reminded the young ones that it was impossible. The important truth for them to remember was that the mountains were not for climbing but for revering. Besides, the range was too far away and the long journey would be fraught with perils. They were admonished to be satisfied with the security of village life and the blessings which the mountains daily bestowed. The entire village attempted to persuade the youngsters to change their minds, but to no avail. To the eager young people the perilous journey seemed only to point out the great learning value of the adventure. They pleaded that the more they could explore the mountains first hand, the more they would revere their beauty and purpose in their lives. Alas, they were forbidden.

The young ones soon departed and began their struggle through the dense forests and unpredictable weather of the mountains. The distance to their goal seemed longer and harder than anticipated. At times they felt they should turn back, but always some inner longing kept them moving ahead. Finally, many weeks later, an exhausted party climbed onto a plateau overlooking the far side of the mountain range. There, to their amazement, were sights unseen by any villager: vast meadows with clear, blue lakes; strange animals grazing among the fruits and berries of the slopes; miles of prairies rolling with wild flowers and grains. But most amazing of all, they were welcomed by people who lived in the meadows and who shared their knowledge of the land. A whole new world opened before them.

Eventually the young people returned down the mountains to their valley. They were anxious to tell the villagers their tales of the sacred mountains. To their utter surprise, they spoke to deaf ears; no one would believe them, for such truths were impossible as well as forbidden.

TWO APPROACHES TO RELIGIOUS CONSCIOUSNESS

Just as there are two ways to approach the mountains in our story, so there are two ways to approach religious consciousness. In either instance, a reverential attitude toward the sacred is preserved, but the distance differs. Most people are inclined to tread the path of religious truth through faith. A few are inclined to search further than faith in hopes of finding concrete experiences that justify their search. This chapter shall explore these two paths.

For the sake of clarification, we shall use distinct terms to show the difference of approach within religious consciousness. It is not a matter of separating believers from unbelievers. Taking the lead from the Jewish and Christian scriptures, one notes that there is a division of teachings that are given to an initiatory group—the school of prophets in the Old Testament and the disciples in the New Testament—while less revealing teachings are given to the ordinary crowd of sincere believers. Although this division of teachings is found consistently throughout, it is not unique to these scriptures. This two-fold approach is found throughout ancient Eastern traditions. For our purposes, the New Testament especially illustrates this division. Jesus speaks parables to the ordinary believers while revealing the mystery or esoteric meanings to his specially chosen followers.

> To you has been given the secret of the Kingdom of God, but for those outside everything is in parables; so that they may indeed see but not perceive, and may indeed hear but not understand...(Mark 4:10)
> He would not speak to them except in parables, but he explained everything to his disciples when they were alone. (Mark 4:34)

This distinction found in scripture formulates the division of religious consciousness guiding this chapter. Thus we have exoteric teachings and esoteric teachings. Exoteric means suitable to be imparted to the public or to the crowd at large. Esoteric means knowledge that is restricted to a small group or understood by specially initiated ones. Throughout the New Testament, there are exoteric teachings presentable to the public and shared by ordinary believers, while another set of teachings, inaccessible to the sincere but ordinary believer, is available only to initiated followers.

THE EXOTERIC BELIEVERS

The conventional exoteric approach to religious truth appeals to the majority of modern Christians. They fill the registered membership of the various denominations. Believers inclined toward the exoteric dimension feel at home among the Bible, the dogmas, beliefs, and rituals. There is an emphasis on communion and fellowship. There are ample sub-organizations within the church structure to allow for social participation and expression of their practical faith. The church bulletin would list a whole gamut of social activities from fund drives and bake sales to scouting, volunteer hospital work, and adult education classes. All these programs invite participation from the church membership. The worship services and social opportunities comprise a large network of religious symbols that unify the faith community. The primary interest of these believers is to support this symbol system that inspires and consolidates their faith. Belonging to a church, taking part in church-sponsored activities, reinforces the faith of the committed believer. Similar motivation would be found among Jewish membership in a synagogue.

The religious testimony of the believers—obvious within the faith community and evident to the citizens of the larger, cultural community— demonstrates the exoteric plane of consciousness. While believers acknowledge an ultimate source—the biblical description of God—they engender religious security and meaning by supporting the symbolic complex that elaborates their unique church affiliation. The Baptist has one way, the Quaker another. The symbols of a preferred denomination—the church's beliefs and activities— define for believers their attitude toward life's expectations. These believers, like the villagers in our story, live within the borders of their beliefs, which define their religious consciousness.

THE ESOTERIC BELIEVER

The esoteric believers usually, but not necessarily, start their spiritual journey from an exoteric stance. They learned and adhered to the conventional beliefs of the denominational community. They envisaged, as far as their spiritual commitment was concerned, a religious destiny completely within the guidelines provided by church authorities and their interpretation of the Bible. Somewhere along their spiritual odyssey, the conventional believers were shaken to the roots of their beliefs. Unforeseen, and certainly unexpected, their religious orientation was challenged: cherished beliefs could not reply to the new questions arising from their life experiences.

This challenge often produces, in the mind and heart of the believers, a spiritual conflict. They want to uphold their allegiance to church beliefs and yet cannot deny that some of life's experiences do not seem to make sense on the basis of their beliefs. Sometimes this perplexing situation in the believer's mind results from a long chain of events, apparently unrelated, but having an accumulative impact upon conventional beliefs. In rare instances, there is such a disruptive experience that the believer almost immediately reorients her/himself in light of the new event.

An example would be the life of the eighteenth-century mystic, Emmanuel Swedenborg. Here was a brilliant scientist, scholar, and political figure of Sweden who had been brought up in the orthodox Lutheran faith of his nation. He underwent a mid-life crisis in his fifties in which his core values were challenged by a series of dreams and visions that overthrew his exoteric faith. In pursuing the meaning of these experiences, Swedenborg was led to reinterpret the significance of Christianity from a perspective based upon his meditational exploration of human consciousness. He still accommodated himself as a church member for many years until an accidental discovery by his minister of his unorthodox beliefs led to his legal persecution. Eventually, he was exonerated in court. Before he predicted his death, he wrote dozens of volumes on his adventures in consciousness, concluding that organized religion was but a stage on one's spiritual journey.

An exceptional conversion of another type is the story of Sundar Singh, who lived in the first part of this century. An Indian Sikh by birth and education, the young Sundar was the sworn enemy of Christ and all

Christians. One evening, to his total surprise, he had a vision of Christ that so overwhelmed him that his basic honesty could not be unimpelled by the genuineness of the spiritual experience. Like St. Paul, Sundar responded immediately to the implications of his vision. It brought such clarity of meaning in his life that he cast aside Sikh orthodoxy to accept Christian baptism. Now an outcast by his community, he spent the rest of his austere life playing out the continuing inspiration of his experience, even residing for training in an ancient cave that belonged to the yogic sages. It is interesting to note that while he accepted Christian baptism, he refused to align himself with any formal church. His message to the world was constructed along the lines of a non-denominational, universal portrait of Jesus Christ.

THE ESOTERIC DISCOVERER

Similarly, the esoteric believer, already an orthodox member of the faith community, undergoes a startling experience that produces a new understanding. The knowledge derived from this experience more vastly exceeds anything learned in the conventional beliefs. Consequently, the believer is no longer comfortable with the quality of knowledge that prevails for an exoteric believer. S/he may remain socially in the church membership, as did Emmanuel Swedenborg, or abruptly depart, as did Sundar Singh. In either case the intelligibility of the experience impels him or her to continue the journey, revising interpretations of life and destiny. The expanding new knowledge does not necessarily annul the content of former beliefs but gives them a more permanent grounding that removes spiritual doubt and provides correction and enlargement where needed.

The following excerpts are descriptions of the esoteric consciousness. These are taken from the acclaimed writings of saints and sages from both the Christian and the yoga traditions.

> Men who are inward and contemplative must go out, according
> to the manner of contemplation, beyond reason and beyond
> discretion; and beyond their created nature, with an everlasting
> beholding in this inborn light, and so they shall become
> transformed, and one with this same light by which they see,

and which they are.... For in this contemplation...he remains free and master of himself in inwardness and in virtue.

Jan van Ruysbroeck (1293-1381)[1]

If I am to know God directly, I must become completely He and He I; so that this He and this I become and are one I.

Meister Eckhart (1260-1329)[2]

Some may ask, what is it to be a partaker of the Divine Nature or a godlike Man? He who is imbued with or illuminated by the Eternal or Divine Light and inflamed or consumed with eternal or divine love, he is a deified man and a partaker of the divine nature.

Anonymous author of the 14th century
Theologica Germanica[3]

I saw God! ...I beheld a fullness and a clearness and felt them within me so abundantly that I cannot describe it, or give any likeness thereof. I cannot say I saw anything corporeal. I beheld the ineffable fullness, but I can relate nothing of it, save that I have seen in it the Sovereign Good.

St. Angela of Foligno (1248-1309)[4]

...how glorious is that soul who has indeed been able to pass from the stormy ocean to Me, the sea pacific, and in that sea, which is myself, the supreme and eternal Deity, to fill the pitcher of her heart.

St. Catherine of Sienna (1347-1380)[5]

The divine dark is the inaccessible light where God is said to dwell. Because transcendent clarity, it is invisible. Because from the heights comes its light, it is inaccessible. All worthy are they who enter there to know and to look upon God. Unseeing and unknowing they attain in truth what is beyond all seeing and all knowing.

Dionysius, (6th century)[6]

That mind is perfect which through true faith, in supreme ignorance supremely knows the supremely knowable, and which, in gazing upon the universe of his handiwork, has received from God comprehensive knowledge of His providence and judgment—but I speak after the manner of men.

St. Maximus (580-662)[7]

Eye cannot see him, nor words reveal him.... When the mind is cleared by the grace of wisdom, he is seen by contemplation, the One without parts.

Maitri Upanishad 6.17[8]

So the wise man, freed from name and form, attains the Supreme divine Person.

Mandaka Upanishad 3.2.8[9]

The external which resides in the soul should be known. Beyond this there is nothing that needs to be known. The enjoyer, the object of enjoyment, the Inspirer—this has been declared to be the All, the threefold Divinity.

Swetasvatara Upanishad 2.15[10]

Contemplating him who has neither beginning, middle nor end, the One, the all-pervading, who is intellect and bliss, the formless, the wonderful...the silent sage reaches the source of Being, the universal witness, on the other shore of darkness.

Kaivalya Upanishad 7[11]

A certain wise man, in search of immortality turned his gaze inward and saw the divine self within.

Katha Upanishad 4.1[12]

Then Naciketas, instructed by Death, having embraced this knowledge and the whole yoga discipline, passed over to the divine and became free from stain and exempt from death;

and so too is anyone who possesses this knowledge of the divine Self within himself.

Katha Upanishad 6.18[13]

The holy soul, when by the inward excitement of its fervor, it is cut off from itself, when it is moved by ecstasy of mind to rise up above itself, when it is carried away altogether and rests in a celestial world, when it is wholly immersed in angelic visions, seems to have transcended the limitations of its native powers.

Richard of St. Victor (d. 1173)[14]

The third step is for the soul to raise itself beyond itself and to strive to see two things: its creator and his own nature. But the soul can never attain to this until it has learned to subdue every image...to reject whatever may come to it through sight or hearing...or any bodily sensation, and to tread it down, so that the soul may see what it itself is outside of its body. After this...let your naked intention fly up above all human reasoning and there you shall find such great sweetness and such great secrets that without special grace there is no one who can think of it except only him who has experienced it.

St. Edmund Rich (1180-1240)[15]

...those things which are known clearly about God and which are beheld by a mind made worthy by exceeding purity, are said to be the glory of God which is seen. So the mind, purified and passing beyond everything material, so that it perfects its contemplation of God, is made divine in what it contemplates.

Origin (185-253)[16]

From a simple reading of these descriptions from Western and Eastern sources, it seems quite obvious that these words could hardly be expressive of denominational beliefs nor conventional piety. If one were to examine a church charter, its prayer books and hymnals, catechisms, or theological manuals, nothing like these descriptions will be found. Nor are these the conceptual results of a theology course. The meaning of these words connote a radical difference from the exoteric mentality.

All of the above Eastern quotations are taken from a group of writings called the *Upanishads*. Their compilation occurred more than three millennia ago, yet their feeling and content surprisingly orients the mind of the reader in the same direction as those descriptions from the Christian writers. One finds in these writings less of a purely rational glorification of God in which abstract or theological terms would be used, than a certain ineffableness. There is diversity of description which does not stand in opposition to each other. Yet in the formal, exoteric teachings of the churches, one would not expect these descriptions; they are too optimistic. The formal separation between man and God, expressing the exoteric distance, collapses. These utterances belong to those who left the valley and climbed the mountain.

ORTHODOX FAITH

As we have seen, there are two orientations to religious consciousness. The esoteric mentality respects the conventional beliefs, dogmas, rites, and other symbols so revered by the exoteric believer. It simply enriches itself beyond them. The typical exoteric believer, however, in allegiance to his/her faith symbols, usually cannot accept any other interpretation.

This rigidity seems uncalled for in that neither rational philosophy nor faith beliefs can completely elucidate the divine. Our senses, nervous system, brain, and discursive mind are primarily oriented to tangible realities and the relations among these realities. People find it more manageable to deal with the stuff and flux of everyday realities, such as working at a job and raising a family, than they do with pondering the subtle intricacies of God's presence in the human soul. While theologians and preachers may remind believers of these spiritual possibilities, the typical believer, living in the humdrum of life, just does not feel that close to these mentioned realities even when accepted in faith. The biblical words are there to inspire and offer solace. Advised by Church authorities, the typical believer, in exoteric faith, neither lives for nor hopes to attain a personal consciousness that would confirm the above quotations.

Nevertheless, the necessity for communication, for soliciting newcomers, for declaring publicly the unique opportunity presented by a believing church requires symbols that express the specific meaning of the church's existence. But as the followers organize and extend their influence to society, their religious symbols assume an adamantine exclusiveness that was unlikely at their inception. Now one is saved, redeemed, baptized, born again, sacramentalized, only in *this* manner and only by *this* church affiliation. The exoteric symbols are so hardened that they have restricted the universality of divine truth and its validity to these definite and finite expressions.

An inflexible tendency develops in the historical progress of a religious tradition, both individually and in community, that hardens the symbols which represent the divine or transcendental realm. The exoteric mentality attributes to a conditioned form—be it a scriptural emphasis, a ritual, a dogma, or pious sentiment—an absoluteness that only the formless and total truth possesses. Consequently, these symbolic forms take on an implacable authority that negates the possibility for truth on any other terms. Better to play safe and believe our way or else risk an irretrievable penalty. At its worst, the religious conclusion amounts to our way or else eternal perdition.

This commandeering incentive is not new. Roman authorities after Caesar felt justified in persecuting the Christians for refusing due reverence to the Roman gods. After 313 A.D., the converted Emperor evened up the score and made it mandatory for all citizens to become Christian. While such religious harassment has diminished in the West, there always resides the possibility for the exoteric symbols to assume a self-sufficiency that will not tolerate exceptions, diversity, or development.

No form can ever be adequate in conveying formless truth. To insist otherwise is to mistake a particular form for the substance. To describe an event of prodigious value (even at a pedestrian level) in a multitude of words, always leaves room for more explanation. If divine truth is intelligible (and otherwise there could be no communication), it cannot be reduced to rational propositions alone. Thus, statements of beliefs may be true, but they cannot close out all other accounts.

The exoteric approach may threaten the possibility for a believer to develop beyond his conventional beliefs. A psychologist interested in religious phenomena, Abraham Maslow, once remarked that "what happens to many people...is that they simply concretize all of the symbols, all of the words, all of the statutes, all of the ceremonies, and by a process of functional autonomy make *them*, rather than the original revelation, into the sacred things and sacred activities. That is to say, this is simply a form of idolatry (or fetishism) which has been the curse of every large religion."[17]

Maslow would not be alone in his criticism. A study of the history of the hundreds of versions of official Christianity would aptly confirm his observation. His telling point: "In idolatry the essential original meaning gets so lost in concretizations that these finally become hostile to the original mystical experiences..."[18]

The exoteric believer, in allegiance to his beliefs, overlooks the primordial origins of religious truth. An attitude of faith, for example, was primary in the disciples until it gave way to its clarifying ground of experience. Faith then becomes secondary and derivative once sufficient experience has occurred. The origin of religious truth that finally nullifies faith-as-ultimate is an unsurpassable experience. This revealing experience unintentionally shatters conventional beliefs and the customary personal and mental limits implied by them. This revelation does not so much contradict as expand the believer's consciousness. The revelatory experience has such stupendous intelligibility about it that both the rational mode of consciousness and the faith mode are, in describing its reality, inadequate but helpful. Encountering disclosures of the absolute defies articulation. What could Moses say about the burning bush and Mount Horeb? What could the disciples report about their Pentecostal event? What can any man or woman utter after an encounter with absolute being?

ESOTERIC REALIZATION

In the esoteric experience, the participant instantly recognizes the impossibility of adequately transferring its meaning into clear, definite and scientific jargon. An event has happened to the person which cannot be located on the familiar horizon of everyday life and customary religious practices. No word or series of symbols can possibly be the exclusive ones that attempt to convey the meaning of the reality. Just as the Eskimo has dozens of words to describe what those living in less wintry conditions would simply label "snow," so does the esoteric mind know the sense of joyous frustration in symbolizing the myriad experience of transcendence.

People do not shop for absolutes in the market place. Instead, the realm of nature and culture is proliferated with specific and limited kinds of things. Our human minds find it comfortable and accessible to engage in particular beings. There are no examples, no precedents, for meeting absolute being. Whatever one attempts to call the revelation, it still exceeds all rational categories. The esoteric, then, who is pursuing this orientation or has encountered the revelatory experience would approach all former beliefs with a recognition of their value but without becoming entrapped in their parochial boundaries.

Having sensed or tasted the revelation, the esoteric person can no longer survive at the level that is comfortable for the exoteric community. Now s/he sees the essential relativity of institutional religions wherever they may prosper on this planet. S/he knows from personal experience that divine truth takes on many guises necessarily for its communication in time and space. The ordinary intelligence does not deal with pure truth, but truth in piecemeal fashion. Conditioned truths imply their unconditional source. The direct revelatory experience of the divine reality has a depth and breadth that simply cannot be totally interpreted from the confinements of mere exoteric beliefs.

By the nature of the experience, no revelation is total. Whether one speaks of Krishna, Moses, Buddha, Jesus, Mohammed, or any sage or saint, what these personages reveal is restricted by their human form. The absolute as such cannot be experienced within finite realities. Divinity as expressed in a human individual, even when the followers identify him as a God, is still not God pure and simple but an embodiment of divinity. In this way, revelation makes divinity available through a living medium which cannot help but limit the presentation. The rational mind, which allows faith in the first place, cannot assimilate a revelatory or transcendental experience. Even religious faith, admitting it as a kind of knowing, cannot assimilate the divine experience. The esoteric's experience is of such a universality that it cannot be focused adequately into the concepts and categories of beliefs or theological statements. These latter speculations about the divine reality cannot satisfy once an immediate and direct experience of unconditioned reality occurs.

The distractions and competitiveness of cultural existence make it difficult to search for the esoteric experience. Those searching for the meaning of life need reminders—beliefs, codes, rituals, scriptures, even taboos—to help sustain their motivation. Yet there remains for most people the assistance of beliefs and dogmas. For most, the achievement requires also a sense of communal support.

CONSCIOUSNESS AND THE ROLE OF TRANSCENDENCE

Spiritual growth is a maturing in the awareness and integration of transcendental reality—conscious awareness of the ultimate source of life. Both the exoteric and the esoteric admit the necessity for symbols of transcendence. The sincere believer acknowledges the existence of transcendental realities by the act of faith in the church's God. This act allows the exoteric believer to have a passive participation in the making of personal beliefs. The purpose of the symbols, however, is to foster growth in the will to believe in the content of the symbols. The act of faith assumes a position of authority that permits the believer to unify everything else in the church. There may yet come unpredictable moments of spiritual stress that test the faith assent. These events "in the vale of tears" will contend, at times, with one's faith commitment. But the meaning of the faith can serve as a consolation in times of stress. To avow, to testify, to participate in sacraments, to witness to the faith becomes in the mind of the believer the symbolic goal of church membership. For believers, faith is all.

The esoteric views the purpose of transcendent symbols as beckoning one beyond their inspiration. Beliefs and dogmas are the road maps that lead one on a voyage—to the conscious realization of transcendental states of reality. The purpose is not to testify to orthodox faith, but to incorporate transcendence into one's lifetime. Consequently, the language of symbols must evoke one to pursue transcendence, not merely believe in it. Belief becomes a tool for exploration and not a secure barrier of scriptural promises.

In yoga philosophy there is a recognition that everyone bears an unrestrictive desire to reach out to transcendence, to render an ultimate explanation to the cosmos. This capacity for unconditional existence becomes articulated differently in religions and societies. Since the adult members of a church have all experienced, one way or another, the persistent urge within themselves to outgrow childish ideas, prejudices, and misinformation, why curtail this fundamental drive at the borders of faith? When faith is put into the context of growth and consciousness, then there would seem to be room for critical development. Since we recognize stages of biological and emotional growth in everyone, could not the same conscious life force continue in its spiritual odyssey to reassess the borders of faith in the hope of enriching new possibilities?

In addition to that level of consciousness that exercises reason and faith, there is a richer, more intuitive perspective. Eckhardt reminds us that we possess a "spark of supersensual knowledge" which is "timeless and spaceless, without any here and now." There, at that level, the esoteric remarks quoted earlier assume their justification. One's objection rises: How can the typical believer propose to attempt such a goal, even if the possibility would exist? It is a matter of priorities. If you want anything out of the ordinary, then you have to make the preparations. How important is this to you? Is there a career, a profession, a vocation whose requirements do not involve rearranging one's habits and preferences? To actualize transcendence could hardly cost less. Finally, the believer must personally decide whether faith and beliefs are there to postpone transcendence or be a goad to its realization.

YOGA FOR PRACTICAL CHRISTIANS

God said, "Let us make humans in our own image, in the likeness of ourselves, and let them be custodians of the fish of the sea, the birds of heaven, the cattle, all the wild beasts and all the reptiles that crawl upon the earth. So God created human beings in the image of God's self, in the image of God they were created, male and female God created them....And God saw all God had made and indeed it was very good." (Genesis 1, 26-27, 31).

It is disconcerting to see how, in general, Christians treat themselves as God's image. In the midst of scientific and technological advancement they are often found wanting in the appreciation of themselves as bodily and spiritual beings. Most Christians tend to ignore the most elementary physiological laws as well as their connection to their spiritual development. Is there a way that preserves the scriptural endorsement of human nature so that Christians can systematically develop themselves in body, mind and spirit?

YOGA'S ORIGIN IS *PHILOSOPHIA PERENNIS*

Among the replies, the ancient science of yoga would respond to this problem by affirming the divine judgment about human nature. As a most positive and comprehensive approach to health and spiritual well-being, yoga confirms the Christian's acceptance of human nature as a priceless gift to be preserved and developed. In yoga one learns to adapt with the seasons, facing life as a whole, developing one's humanity to its fullest potential. For a Christian, the techniques and philosophy of yoga can serve as an invitation to foster the biblical injunction to perfect oneself as God's image.

The science of yoga belongs to an ancient source of perennial wisdom. The school of yoga that embraces both the theoretical and experiential dimensions of human nature is called *raja* yoga, or "the royal path." It is a holistic tradition among the schools of yoga for it regards, among other things, physical health, diet, exercise, the development of virtue, the regulation of breath, the ordering of emotions, concentration, and the development of intuitive awareness. Unless otherwise noted, when we speak of yoga throughout this chapter, we will be referring to the royal path.

As a science, yoga has become increasingly recognized in the Western world, but often Christians mistake it for an Eastern religion. Yoga and Christianity are like two streams flowing from the same fountain of perennial wisdom. Each has a different approach in assisting human development. Like Christianity, yoga is broader than any one culture. To speak of yoga as a wisdom means that it transcends cultural labels, that it shares with other wise traditions a timeless quality that makes it a continual resource for human enrichment.

Yoga, then, is not an Eastern import. It is not a religion, nor an ethnic custom. That its traditional ground for thousands of years has been the Himalayan mountain region was a geographical advantage to its founders and not a boundary to its universality. Yoga remains free of ethnic, religious, political, or social influence. Christianity shares an Eastern origin with yoga and likewise transcends both geographical and cultural boundaries that initially supported it. Does one speak of the circulation of the blood or the law of gravity as being Eastern or Western? Much less should anyone subscribe to yoga or Christianity on the mistaken association that they are indigenous to the Eastern world.

As a non-cultural contribution to human development, yoga is applicable to any citizen of any country. It is concerned about the basics of human nature as such. Christianity likewise offers universal values that inspire humankind without jeopardizing the cultural preferences of believers. Both yoga and Christianity share a common appreciation of human nature and its destiny that has a timeless character enabling their common vision to be implemented throughout history. They can be considered two paths joined in illuminating man's ignorance with the one light of sacred knowledge.

The classic scripture that reveals the heart of *raja* yoga is called *The Yoga Sutras of Patanjali*. The word *sutra* means "thread" and refers to the 196 aphorisms that comprise the codification of the centuries-old wisdom. These aphorisms are like jewels threaded together to form a beautiful necklace of practical truth. The *sutras* were written in a language that makes statements about the spiritual development of human nature without relying upon cultural or religious symbols. These systemic affirmations analyze the various powers and faculties of human consciousness both in themselves and as they coherently relate to the body and the environment. In addition, Patanjali indicates the technical exercises that actually prove the theoretical proposition enumerated. By reading the text, one is given a tour through the human mind in its pursuit of spiritual excellence. By performing these *sutras* under the direction of a competent teacher, one has a step-by-step manual for achieving the goal of complete human integration.

To put Christian minds at ease, it is important to remember that yoga does not displace religion. Yoga can no more threaten genuine religious beliefs than can a basic course in animal husbandry. Yoga's interest lies in the study of human nature and its unfoldment from the primary perspective of consciousness. It investigates questions concerned with the range of the human mind's powers, the energy interrelationship between mind and body, and the healthy attitudes one should have in order to cope with life calmly and intelligently. These and other similar questions are treated extensively by its philosophy and psychology.

YOGA OFFERS A HEALTHY CRITIQUE OF SOCIETY

For society, yoga poses a critique of culture. Whenever society becomes complacent or discouraged with its current level of civilization, yoga quietly insists upon a special feature of human nature. No matter how bogged down or overwhelmed we may become with our involvement in society, we possess, according to yoga philosophy, a transcendental nature. In spite of our needless worries and tribulations, yoga reminds us that we are more than our body, our mind, our career, our success or failure with life, for we possess a center of wisdom and strength within that makes our nature wider than any travail that may temporarily overcome us.

In yoga philosophy, a distinction is made between human nature and human culture. People cannot help but identify with their ethnic origins or national territory. As a result, they forget that these qualifications denote, like the chopsticks of China or the saris of India, only a cultural preference. Within a society, cultural protocol only expresses the imaginative art of human communication; it cannot disclose universal insight for human development. Cultural customs are only temporary; they cannot resolve the quest for human happiness. On the other hand, yoga, being outside cultural frameworks, addresses itself to the root problems of life and the means to human fulfillment.

We all live in culture and history. We grow accustomed to our habits and cannot easily avoid being provincial and sectarian in our desires. Yoga recognizes that beneath the multitude of desires within the human soul there lies a fundamental one that is rarely satisfied—a desire to know experientially the ultimate meaning of human existence and the nature of human happiness.

What human existence means to you may not be what it means to me. This is true as long as we are speaking from a relative perspective. But is there a broader perspective, one that satisfies everyone regardless of race, creed or locale?

If one speaks in ultimates, there cannot be a diversity of goals. There may be, however, a diversity of means to achieve one goal. If the case were otherwise, if your version of ultimate human existence were opposite mine, yet equally true, then there would be two human natures. Your nature would be type A, while mine would be type Z. We could not speak of the human family as being one. To some extent, people already practice this shortcoming by focusing prejudicially on those factors that make them different from others. The unity of the human family, in essence, is not separated by those factors or items that make someone different from his neighbor. Race, color, creed, bank account, vacation home are only relative features. They unfortunately impede appreciation of the basic unity of the living organisms called human.

The differences in personality are obvious but this amazing variety still does not prevent thoughtful reflection from discerning a common nature shared by all. Appraised of cultural differentiations, people still uphold themselves as one human family, one kind of being. The paradox is that individual actions do not always substantiate this universal truth. Thus wars continue.

YOGA'S TEN CHARACTER COMMITMENTS

In its study of human nature, yoga outlines its remarks from a universal perspective. It does not explain how to be a better carpenter or investment banker. It goes deeper and explains how the carpenter's or the banker's same human nature can reach its inner potential.

These investigations of human faculties contribute to the psychological and moral heritage found in moral philosophy. The Christian understanding of the moral and intellectual virtues (Latin *vir/virtus*, meaning "power") is complemented by the *Sutras'* analysis of these same innate powers. These powers are disciplined, in the yoga analysis, by foundational attitudes that are naturally fostered in action by those who are striving to live humane lives. Yoga encourages the development of these attitudes as ten commitments (called the *yamas* and *niyamas*) to support the individual's growth towards self-realization. The five *yamas* guide one's relationship with other beings. They are:

> *ahimsa*—the art of non-violence in thought, word, and deed
> *satya*—the art of truthfulness toward others
> *asteya*—the art of non-stealing
> *brahmacharya*—the art of sexual continence
> *aparigraha*—the art of non-attachment

The five *niyamas* guide one's attitude towards personal conduct. They are:

saucha—the art of purity that leaves one's mind unfettered by
prejudicial thoughts and one's body hygienically clean
santosha—the art of contentment under all circumstances
tapas—the art of spiritual fervor
swadhyaya—the art of self-discovery
Ishwara pranidhana—the art of acknowledging the divinity
within

These maturing attitudes comprise the ingredients that foster an
integration of character, which, in turn, disposes the aspirant for creative
enterprises that lead to self-realization. They can guide the aspirant in the face
of unruly impulses and negative evaluations. Unless one learns to foster
positive attitudes in meeting life's challenges, the natural powers of mental and
physical energy may turn self-destructive. In examining these guidelines one
can find only a healthy and sound regard for cultivating human potentials.

AN OPERATIONAL SCIENCE

The ancient science of yoga endorses all the operative principles of human
nature that stimulate optimal fulfillment. Understanding yoga is not like
studying Grey's anatomy classic. The emphasis of yoga is on the dynamic
utilization of human nature. Right at the start, it parts company from various
fields of theoretical study by insisting that it cannot be authentically
understood except as a dynamic discipline. Yoga is yoga and understood as
yoga only in the act of applying it. The meaning of yoga dawns not from
reading about it but in its performance.

Yoga's emphasis on breathing is a case in point. It does not treat breathing
from a static point of view. As an overlooked aspect of human nature,
breathing as a subject of study offers little stimulation for reflection. Yet the
rate, depth, and rhythm of one's breath constantly influence the way one feels,
the thoughts one thinks and the zest with which one faces life. Everyone
breathes the same air with similar organs, but not everyone enjoys the optimal
benefits from proper breathing. Yoga science recognizes that breathing is not a
theoretical reflection but an activity that engages the entire metabolic and
emotional constitution of the breather. Discovering that breath affects the

whole nature of man, the yoga sages probed the mystery of breathing by practicing different techniques for different effects upon their persons. They realized that specific exercises in breathing unify the mind and body into a healthier relationship.

By practicing a simple form of diaphragmatic breathing one comes to know through that experience alone that a beneficial change has taken place in one's overall feeling and thinking. The act of proper breathing promotes a coordination between the body and mind that is unobtainable by other methods. The healthy end result is there because the laws of breathing, rooted in one's nature and properly stimulated, produce definite effects upon one's being. These effects have been verified under controlled experimentations. Thus the laws of breathing, discovered by yoga practitioners, are not the result of authoritative decrees or faith pronouncements; they remain the positive truths of using human nature according to its inherent laws. This is why yoga belongs to the heritage of human wisdom.

From the continued practice of yogic breathing, one's self-understanding increases. One is not merely exchanging gases. The experiential performance of breathing improves the practitioner's sensitivity to their inner nature. A kind of inner learning, an experiential feedback, emerges during the focused practice. One gains an awareness of controlling and studying nature in a direct and immediate sense—a dynamic knowledge rather than a theoretical concept. An academic knowledge of the human respiratory system cannot provide this assuring knowledge nor alter one's physical and spiritual condition. Yet knowing the respiratory system through the act of breathing—a different kind of operational knowing than reflecting on abstract concepts—generates a self-knowledge that is unavailable to the manual description of breathing.

Yoga establishes its rightful claim to true knowledge through practice, not through intellectual coherence. Verification of its worth is first-hand knowledge, always made by the individual doing the practice. One can immediately submit a particular practice to personal and scientific scrutiny. To embark on the practice of yoga is to enter, not a speculative tour of ideas, but an adventure in transformative living for which one accepts responsibility.

Obviously, yoga can be described with concepts. In addition to the *Sutras*, the reflected ideas of yoga are systematically and coherently outlined in another text: *Samkhya Karika*. The concept of yoga, however, is not the contact with its truth. Yoga's power comes not from the idea but from the actual use of the interior laws of man's nature. Like Christianity, which makes sense only when it is put into action, yoga postulates that people carry within themselves the impulse or appetite towards self-actuality. Men and women want to actualize their total nature, to experience life as richly, as enjoyably, as maturely as possible. The personal troubles they encounter, including emotional distress and disease, are symptomatic of their need to regulate and develop this inherent appetite for life.

Yoga further recognizes that human nature is multileveled, a complex combination of vegetative, sentient, rational, and intuitional forces that can function organismically for well-being. The inability to achieve this integrated condition as an abiding state results primarily from many impedances, especially the suffering of ignorance. Yoga treats suffering ultimately as the temporary product of men and women's failure to understand themselves. It can be eradicated through the discipline of true knowledge about the operations of their nature. For overcoming suffering, all the dimensions of consciousness and all the levels of physical embodiment must become involved as a holistic enterprise.

Yoga, therefore, is an exercise in applied philosophy. This definition, however, departs from the modern conception of philosophy as only a theoretically coherent reflection upon life. Yoga's purpose is not to arrive at correct concepts in order to satisfy the intellect, but rather to postulate guidelines for engaging one's latent potentials and unify them for ultimate well-being. With that aim in mind, and on that basis alone, should yoga fail or pass.

Christians, in pondering the path of yoga, can discover a resource of practical knowledge that will provide an integration of body, mind, and spirit for fulfilling the purpose of life.

YOGA AND THE SERMON ON THE MOUNT

The Sermon on the Mount expresses the mind of Jesus more clearly than any other scriptural proclamation. It is a distillation of wisdom that summarizes his vision of the nature of human relationships and the attitudes of mind and heart for fulfilling human destiny. It is one of the most challenging programs for spiritual development elaborated in the history of spirituality. It is a public manifesto for Christian identity. In short, it is the criterion by which the world ought to judge the value of Christianity.

The written gospel words that came down to believers fifty years after Jesus' sermon have accumulated an expansion of meaning in the communities in which they were repeated. We are fortunate in having before us the final editing of those words. Although the Sermon was given in Judaic-Roman culture, there are metaphors and symbols that ring out in the hearts of all people a message of liberation and fulfillment.

Every book needs an interpreter. The text of the Sermon is no exception in relying upon interpretive tools. Textual analysis relies upon many professional fields of knowledge in order to explicate the meaning. Philological studies, cultural archaeology, even economics and sociological knowledge are used by exegetes and theologians for elucidating the significance of biblical passages. Everyone gains from this collaboration.

Theologians always borrow some framework for explication. After the Apostles, the Church Fathers used various rational disciplines such as Greek philosophy and psychology to elaborate the implications of the Gospels. Later Christian writers like Augustine used Platonic philosophy. In the high middle ages Saint Thomas Aquinas used Aristotle's works for elaborating biblical texts. Modern theologians like Bultmann, Tillich, and Rahner show their reliance upon the philosophical thought of Martin Heidegger. In almost every instance it can be shown that biblical scholars and theologians utilized the sciences and knowledge at their disposal for opening the Bible wider to its readers. Any science or body of knowledge that shares a common subject matter with the Bible is a valuable aid as far as it goes with the investigation of biblical texts.

As a scientific tool for investigating human consciousness and for discerning various states of mind as evidenced in the Bible, yoga qualifies for this task. Christians who study and practice yoga will soon find that their efforts are complementary with many Christian insights that aid in the pursuit of spiritual growth.

In this chapter certain yoga terms and explanations will be offered to focus an appreciation of biblical themes and passages. Biblical revelation is not a random event, for its discernment presupposes a certain awareness, whether in a Moses, an Esther, a Jesus, or a Paul. And for the truths of the Bible to have universal import, the understanding of revelation cannot be separated from one's level of self-understanding. One receives what one is prepared to receive. Here the Bible and yoga presuppose the same internal dimension for reception. While there are many valid approaches to studying the Sermon, such as from the standpoint of theology, morality, literary composition, or historically, our concern will be an analysis from the standpoint of yoga psychology.

THE TWO SERMONS

What we know today as the Sermon on the Mount is ascribed to two writers, Matthew and Luke, in two separate versions. The more familiar version is found in Matthew's Gospel (Matthew 5:1-7:29); it is also the more descriptive. Luke's account (Luke 6: 20-49) actually takes place on a plain after Jesus descended the mountain. Matthew's broader version includes many of Jesus' later teachings on Hebrew law which were given to the crowds. This inclusion would be necessitated by the fact that Matthew's audience was primarily Jewish. These later passages are not included in Luke's version of the Sermon because Luke wrote for Gentile converts. They knew their audiences.

We should not be surprised by these and other omissions when the Gospels are compared. Each Gospel, after all, was gathered from and prepared for a distinctly different audience. Matthew's concern was for Jewish converts to Christianity. His reliance upon the Law, the prophets, and the writings (the threefold division of the Hebrew Bible) would necessarily be required of his listeners to appreciate that Jesus is the Torah's fulfillment. In Matthew's Gospel Jesus is the new lawgiver, fulfilling the role of Moses as well as being the new David, the prince of the new kingdom. Obviously Matthew will connect as many of the Old Testament figures and passages to the career of Jesus as possible.

Luke, on the other hand, would not be interested in the Hebrew configurations since he could not presuppose familiarity with Jewish customs and practices in his audience, and they might even have been a source of alienation at the time. Yet modern Christians cannot help but feel inspirational power revealed by these passages.

The scene for the Sermon portrays Jesus distancing himself from the crowds and teaching, not standing as was expected of a Jewish teacher, but sitting as characteristic of a master/disciple relationship. Lest we forget, he spoke not to the crowds but specifically to his disciples. "Seeing the crowds, he went up the mountain. There he sat down and was joined by his disciples. Then he began to speak. This is what he apprentised them" (Matthew 5:1). Scriptural research indicates that the Sermon was meant exclusively for Jesus' disciples and not for the general public. Luke's account supports the theory that the Sermon was meant only for the disciples. According to Luke, the Sermon begins, "Then fixing his eyes on his disciples, Jesus said..." (Luke 6:20). That emphasis, however puzzling, is crucial.

In the Sermon Jesus describes the nature of the optimal disciple. He attempts to convey the spirit of his New Law which should animate the aspirant. Later, as the scene was recounted in the Christian communities, the Christians were inspired by this portrait in hopes of being imbued with the same spirit. The Sermon indicates much more than moral qualities associated with a civil character. It indicates a total spiritual transformation.

THE BEATITUDES

Jesus' Sermon begins with his description of the beatitudes. He is actually relating Old Testament wisdom and placing it in a new context. If one were to read in the prophet Isaiah Chapter 1 and the Psalms 1:1, 32:1, and 41:2, one could get a sense of the continuity of insight that Jesus is conveying to his students.

Every beatitude starts with the word "blessed." Blessed indicates a condition of good fortune or good prospects. Since the kingdom will be everlasting, the notion of "blessed" includes more than a temporal condition. A blessing, on the other hand, can be a temporary enjoyment, as often is the case in many passages of the Torah or the Old Testament. There the follower of Yahweh may enjoy good health, prosperous economy, abundant crops and herds. Yet this good fortune is transitory. It's good while it lasts. In Jesus' words, however, the blessing conveys a certain permanency, for these are the qualifications for the reign of the kingdom of God.

Let us now take a brief look at the beatitudes. Although Luke's account lists only four beatitudes (and four curses), since these are also listed by Matthew, we shall pursue Matthew's longer version, which is also more common to modern Christians.

First Beatitude: "Blessed are the poor in spirit for theirs is the kingdom of heaven." The poor in spirit indicates an interior purification of desires for sensible things. Objective wealth is of no concern. The phrase underscores an attitude of inner detachment from external possessions. One of the essential qualities recorded by the *Yoga Sutras* for achieving spiritual growth is *vairagya*, an abiding sense of detachment from craving external things. This quality of the human spirit recognized by the *Sutras* is endorsed universally among spiritual teachers. The average mind becomes distracted by the array of sensory wares provided in one's culture. A certain inner distancing from an otherwise healthy ambition for possessions needs to be integrated in order to sustain a wholesome, spiritual perspective. Likewise a subtlety enters the aspirant's path as he strives to attain spiritual advancement. Here, too, one must have a higher degree of detachment from the tendency to flatter oneself in spiritual progress. Detachment keeps a feeling for one's spiritual need. And so the poor in spirit will one day inhabit the kingdom.

Second Beatitude: "Blessed are the gentle, for they shall inherit the earth." This passage is a repetition of Psalm 37:11 where the meaning conveys a gentle or considerate disposition: "The humble shall have the land for their own to enjoy untroubled peace." In the biblical mind the land was a divine inheritance given by God to his faithful ones. Thus, to possess the land meant to possess God. Gentleness indicates an attitude of nonviolence, the *ahimsa* of the *Yoga Sutras*. Amidst the unexpected changes and pressures of life, there are many occasions for losing one's temper or becoming upset. Not only does this provoke violence upon one's nervous system, it creates a habit of mind that can usurp social relations. Gentleness is a sign of strength. It means one can cope with the vagaries of life with a gentle hand. Gentleness presumes great discipline; thus the gentle ones stand ready to receive their spiritual inheritance.

Third Beatitude: "Blessed are those who mourn, for they shall be comforted." People often mourn over a failure, a task or project that should have worked out. Jesus himself was no stranger to this kind of mourning: "My heart is nearly broken with sorrow" (Matthew 26:38). There are times when even the best of plans will not materialize, when injustice, privation, and death itself seem to snatch at our happiness. What this beatitude seems to be affirming is that even this sorrow shall also pass, and that an everlasting comfort awaits the soul.

Fourth Beatitude: "Blessed are those who hunger and thirst for righteousness, for they shall be satisfied." In the Old Testament one hungers and thirsts for the word of God. The personal possession of the word produces righteousness by placing believers in the attitude for conducting themselves according to the spirit of the word. The biblical notion of hunger and thirst would be an illustration of the fundamental appetite for truth which is the basis for yoga's quest as well. People in all walks of life ultimately want to know the truth;

they are unsatisfied with anything less. Jesus is building upon this natural exigency by showing how those who sustain it, who are true to it, will one day be satiated with nothing less than fullness of divine truth. The desire for righteousness places the disciple in the attitude of conducting thought and action according to the divine spirit within.

Fifth Beatitude: "Blessed are the merciful, for they shall obtain mercy." In the Old Testament it is written: "Shall a man refuse mercy to his fellows and yet seek pardon for his own sins?" (Sirach 28:4). To the Hebrew mind the theme of showing mercy is always a sign of God's mercy towards humanity. One shows mercy because one has experienced mercy. The concern and care for the welfare of others is precisely the foundation of *raja* yoga, for the very first quality of spirit that the *yamas* build upon is *ahimsa*, which means "non-harming," its positive side being compassion. Hence we find in Buddhist yoga that compassion is the highest virtue. Were not the Christians known by how much they loved one another? Empathy with the poor and the weak indicates a relationship between the doing of mercy and the receiving of mercy. This direct cause-effect relationship corresponds to the concept of *karma* in yoga and in the Gospels. Compassion at the human level reveals the highest form of love.

Sixth Beatitude: "Blessed are the pure in heart, for they shall see God." To the Jewish mind it was impossible to look upon God and live. Here Jesus shockingly reverses this belief and insists that seeing God is a possibility. One need only be unprejudiced in heart. Pure hearts have nothing whatsoever to do with purity from sin or even chastity. Purity is rather an integrity of outlook motivated by noble principles—the magnanimous person. The same individual is mentioned in the Torah as the "righteous" or the "just" one. These are the ones who respond fully to God's gift of life, for only these can express an unbounded generosity of spirit. This generosity of spirit prepares consciousness for experiencing higher realities. "When the mind is purified, God is seen in the silence of meditation" (Mundaka Upanishad, 3.1.8). The same insight is proffered in *Sutras* 2:41 where from mental purity arises perfect self-knowledge.

Seventh Beatitude: "Blessed are the peacemakers, for they shall be called sons of God." Peace, according to Augustine, signifies the tranquility of order. Order is not a static term. To preserve the order of life requires a dynamic commitment calling upon all one's enemies. Throughout the Gospels God is portrayed as a God of peace; Jesus himself is described as the prince of peace. The notion of sonship indicates a perfect communion with God. With that ordered relationship prevailing between God and human, one can be a doer of peace. Likewise, the practice of yoga produces a new sense of order within, for yoga is the middle path between extremes. The integration of mind, body, and spirit through spiritual practices recovers a sense of tranquility that can be borne to others. The whole effort of the Jewish notion "son of God" expressed a mission of restoration. The end result of that restoration is peace.

Eighth Beatitude: "Blessed are those who are persecuted for righteousness' sake, for theirs is the kingdom of heaven." Both Jesus and his followers encountered persecution. While they did not seek to alienate others, they managed to incur all forms of opposition to their projects. A lifestyle of integrity and honesty may not always be appreciated in every social environment. Only those striving to be poor in spirit are equipped to withstand persecution that may inadvertently arise from following one's conscience. And yet there is no other way but to follow the impulse of truth and continue to give compassion to others. These are the credentials of one who is eligible for the kingdom.

THE NEW LAW OF INNER TRANSFORMATION

The beatitudes are expressions of the inner transformation that must take root in order for one to participate in the kingdom. These characteristics, which constitute the unfolding of the awakened personality, are the evidence that one has active citizenship in the kingdom. The values espoused by the beatitudes exceed Wall Street's standard for success. For all its worth, the technological world cannot satisfy the disciple once his inner spirit aims at achieving perfection. For those who have yet to experience the full entry into the kingdom, the beatitudes offer an encouraging inspiration amidst their human condition.

When the spirit of the kingdom animates the disciple, the characteristics of the beatitudes will be detectable by other people. In this way the disciple becomes the "salt of the earth" and the "light of the world" (Matthew 5:13-16) as instructed by Jesus after he spoke them in his Sermon.

Already the scriptures had recognized that salt prevented corruption in many perishable foods (Leviticus 2:13, Ezekiel 43:24). As a condiment it was irreplaceable (Job 6:6). The Book of Sirach even considers it one of the "elements necessary for man's life" (Sirach 30:26).

The passage applying "light" to the disciples is an Old Testament borrowing. Israel was the light to the nations (Isaiah 42:6); the servant of Yahweh was called the same (Isaiah 49:6). Jesus also applied it to himself (John 8:12) and extended it to his followers (John 12:35, Luke 2:32).

Thus the injunctions for being salt and light are not stressing the performance of missionary activity as much as sustaining an integrity of spirit. One will be successful in the eyes of Jesus precisely because he remains faithful to his new uprightness. On this basis can he truly be an active force purifying and leading others to enlightenment.

The transformation of the disciples into their new uprightness actually crowns and prolongs the norms of the Old Testament. Jesus takes the moral norms of the Mosaic law and extends them by insisting upon their interior character. People may follow sound moral laws by rote, without actually assimilating them into their own spirit. In verses 21-48 of the Sermon, Jesus selects some moral prescriptions from the law and shows in six examples how these are now to be conducted by his transformed disciples. True morality emerges when the human spirit consciously accepts its own inherent ideals.

Under the Old Law one refrained from murder. Under Jesus' New Law there must be no anger, no insulting remark. This admonition aligns Jesus with *ahimsa*, non-violence. One does not come to God without first reconciling himself to his fellow men. Instead of multiplying oaths to God, let us now have unfeigned sincerity with one another. While Jesus enumerates only a few concrete examples, the import of his meaning is obvious. Unless human acts manifest from one's humane ideals, these prescriptions cannot be fulfilled.

The *ius talionis* (an eye for an eye), for example, was inbred in the Middle East. It was considered an act of cowardice not to return vengeance for injustice committed against the tribe. Jesus is not preventing one from resisting an unjust attack nor eliminating injustice to society; he refuses to condone someone's reaction out of vengeance or returning evil for evil. Retaliation must now give way to a higher justice.

THE IMPOSSIBLE GOAL: FOLLOW YOUR NATURE AS THE FATHER DOES HIS

In his Sermon, Jesus brings love of neighbor to its summit: include your enemy. His phrase is a dramatic way of expressing a profound truth, that is, love everyone. Here is the hallmark of Christianity, a *bhakti* path. For someone to express universal love, to become humanly what God is divinely, affects, according to Jesus, a profound union with the divine. One enters on equal footing with Jesus himself: "You will be sons of your Father in heaven" (Matthew 5:45). The power of universal love, which includes even enemies, now presents human beings as the fulfilled images of the heavenly Father.

Finally, Jesus announces the paradoxically impossible: be perfect as your Father is perfect (Matthew 5:48). The standard of achievement, the criterion of performance, is nothing less than the realization of your essence. Human ingenuity, high moral standards, Nobel peace prizes, all fade into insignificance with this outrageous demand. No less is expected of the disciples than a fidelity to their transcendental nature.

All the beatitudinal qualities could be reasonably appreciated as ideals to strive towards and eventually achieve. The final instruction, however, to become perfect seems beyond human capability. Jesus seemingly demands an impossible quest. Christian morality is rigorous enough, but is he not requiring transcendental elevation?

Perhaps Jesus' assertion should be taken as a simile? The context of the Sermon will not allow for this diminishing interpretation. A sense of the impossible conclusion fits the pattern of Jesus' thoughts. As unpredictable as his statements may be, they are nonetheless not inconsistent with his earlier demands.

For many church-affiliated Christians, the Sermon on the Mount stands upon an untouchable pedestal of human conduct, an inspiring motif but hardly achievable. The paradox remains: how can frail human beings in their wildest imaginings compare their potential with the infinite resources of the creator?

THE KINGDOM HIDDEN IN PARABLES

In helping to resolve this incredible impasse, let us recall some important clues throughout the New Testament. One discovers, first of all, in reading all the Gospels, that Jesus preferred to explain his message only to the disciples. The same message was offered to the public in cryptic parables. Understanding parables is like solving riddles: one needs the key. But the key was never handed to the public. This omission does not receive the significance today that it possessed in Jesus' time. Was he being discriminatory or can we give him the benefit of the doubt?

Every Christian and biblical scholar recognizes the importance of Jesus' message for the world. Whether one describes the message as salvation, redemption, liberation, glorification, or resurrection, these are simply partial attempts to reveal the basic overall proclamation: the kingdom of God is at hand. Keeping this unparalleled good news in mind, one still finds that the kingdom is never explained. Its significance remains a secret, couched in enigmatic phrases that elude the general public. This is not a private evaluation but precisely the judgment the Gospels narrate about the matter.

> When he was alone, the twelve, together with the others who formed his company, asked what the parables meant. He told them, "the secret of the kingdom of God is given to you but to those who are outside everything comes in parables" (Mark 4:10-11).

A careful examination of the Gospel parables shows that out of the sixty-three parables of Jesus, forty-one parables are explained—twenty-eight to the disciples, but only thirteen to the crowds. At the same time twenty-two are not explained at all—seven left unexplained for the disciples, but fifteen left unexplained for the crowd. Those parables concerned with the kingdom are never explained to the crowd.

Matthew records a conversation that the disciples had with Jesus about his reluctance to explain the kingdom to the interested crowd:

> Then the disciples went up to him and asked, "Why do you talk to them in parables?" "Because," he replied, "the mysteries of the kingdom of heaven are revealed to you, but they are not revealed to them" (Matthew 13:10-11).

The use of the word "mystery" here is identical in the text with the word "secret" used above in the quotation from Mark. The meaning of mystery or secret refers to the divine transcendental knowledge of the kingdom. It does not mean that the kingdom is unintelligible, but that the metaphor's significance exceeds rational analysis. Mystery thus indicates such richness of truth that the rational mode of understanding cannot grasp it.

IS THE KINGDOM CLOSED TO ORDINARY CHRISTIANS?

The question comes to this: if neither the crowds understood nor the Gospels exposed the kingdom, where does that leave ordinary followers? To say that Jesus himself is the secret does not really answer the question. Jesus quite obviously taught certain truths which affected his disciples in a radical manner. Equally, not everyone who believed in Jesus could perform as the disciples. To know the mystery was to possess the key to the kingdom. From examining the lifestyle of Jesus and his training of the disciples this knowledge could not be mere information.

Jesus knew the mystery and could lead others into the kingdom. Apparently, the mystery-knowledge could not be conveyed in ordinary expressions. Parables could help because of their symbolic characteristics. There is more knowledge in a parable than the surface meaning exposes. The words of a parable have some relationship to their common experience but simultaneously the full meaning passes beyond the ordinary, rational interpretation. The words may appear so enigmatic that the mind cannot fathom any meaning, or the interpretative possibilities are perplexingly so broad that a definite assurance of meaning eludes the mind.

Being an Eastern teacher, Jesus teaches not for the sake of intellectual satisfaction, but to engage the whole person. Reading the Gospels is not a very intellectually exciting task. No doubt the passages reflect Jesus as quite intelligent, but his efforts in teaching were not to convey ideas alone, but the deepest truths of life: What is the purpose of existence? What is human destiny? How does one attain it? What is the true nature of divinity? These were the kinds of questions that he provoked in his audiences. To assimilate his teachings was to accept a change in one's life. Growth-oriented, personalistic development, healthy self-image—all these contemporary terms—could partially apply to his method. These applications are utterly insufficient, however, without the prior understanding of the mystery of the kingdom.

Jesus remarks that whoever has ears to hear will hear. The truths of the Sermon will be intelligible only to those who have the capacity to understand. His remark points up the relationship between the knower and the ability to discern the reality represented in symbolic form. The kingdom is not real estate. The reading of the texts allude to an inner reality not readily perceptible by the crowds. If this interpretation has merit, then the ability to discern the kingdom's meaning would bear directly upon the disposition of the human spirit.

Knowledge is always a function of the being of the knower. To alter the capacity to know, the very nature of the knower must change. Taking courses at school does not affect the inner capacity of one's nature. School provides information and perhaps an improvement in the skills of thinking. The ordinary, natural, everyday mode of knowing is discursive: reflective thinking. As long as one identifies with the discursive manner of knowing, as long as one thinks that rational thinking is the highest activity for grasping reality, then the kingdom remains closed. Even faith in the kingdom does not gain more for the believer. Belief in the kingdom merely alleges that the kingdom exists, but does not disclose its secrets. Belief, like reason, finds only circumstantial hints and clues. Neither is able to resolve the mystery.

To return to the conduct of those who can manifest the beatitudes, there is a relationship between their inner state and the outer activity in human action. To demonstrate the behavior of the Sermon in their daily lives, the disciples require an interior state of mind and heart that supercedes but does not nullify the normal virtues of good citizenship. As mentioned, the actions of any nature flow from the being of that nature. In order for the disciples to live the Sermon, their inner nature had to change. Whether one calls it growth, evolution, or expansion, the inner dynamics of knowing and loving had to undergo a drastic increase. This inner change cannot be equated with an intellectual broadening of the mind. The secret of the kingdom is not a fascinating new concept. To acquire new ideas about the world or self or even God cannot account for the behavior recognized in one possessing the beatitudes, understanding the parables, being a self-conscious son or daughter of the Father, performing wonders, and demonstrating perfection.

In describing the kingdom, Jesus is not talking about an idyllic territory. The kingdom is his symbolic expression for an inner transformation of spirit— what the Gospels call the "new man," the reborn event (the Fundamentalists portray it differently). To transform the nature of man or woman is to bring the potentials of mind and heart, those cognitive and affective dimensions, into a superior actuality. The being of the person undergoes a metamorphosis. An interior change of this magnitude is associated with a radical, constitutional intensification of the life principle within the person. One's life power increases exponentially.

THE KINGDOM AS THE AWAKENED LIFE FORCE

In understanding yoga as a sacred science, the human, individual life force is known as *devatma shakti*. As the life force intensifies, so the emergent cognitive and affective aspects of one's nature change accordingly. With the life force stimulated into new abundance, it radically expands one's ability to know, love, and behave. Even more than a myopic person beginning to have normal vision, or someone with lifelong color blindness suddenly perceiving colored objects, the conscious powers of one's being are so enormously amplified that the former capacities appear to be a lesser nature. Scripture refers to this former state as "the old Adam."

The kind of qualitative change demanded for the perfect disciple's performance is truly accomplishable provided the *shakti,* or the latent life force within, activates. An analogy to biological evolution is pertinent here. The human organism grows from the tiniest embryo into adulthood. That tiny seed invisibly bears all the potentials that comprise the adult, but in latency. Human growth means that the various potentials of the life force are being actualized, and the ability to use its power is available. What is not actualized remains dormant. Reaching voting age, for example, does not mean we have exhausted our total potential in mind, body, and especially in spirit. In fact, we may not even have the ability to vote intelligently.

Spiritual development as known in ancient traditions has a definite, evolutionary order to it. The expansion of *shakti* does not happen mechanically or in a haphazard manner. A disciple undergoes a long preparation, for the amplified energy of life must find the properly tilled soil in which to grow or harm results. Since human nature utilizes a body, the necessary physical and cognitive preparations are indispensable. Mind and body cooperate in this transmutation.

With the intensification of the life force, latent powers of the human spirit reveal themselves, thus challenging one's previous assumptions about self-limitations. Jesus remarked that he came to give life in abundance. Life is something to experience. And certainly the Gospel accounts show that the disciples were led through life experiences that finally altered their self-understanding.

The increase in the life force, controlled and directed, leads to *sacra sophia*, holy knowledge, an understanding of "heaven and earth." This phenomenon is reflected in the water initiation of Jesus. Here the ascetic John leads Jesus through a consciousness-raising event. The passages about the heavens opening and the dove of peace descending are symbolic insertions from the Genesis account of creation which describe the cosmic power of consciousness to manifest its creativity. As applied to the initiation story, the same creative life force transfuses through Jesus, producing a cosmic awareness. Jesus understands his nature and the range of his powers through this experience. Living in Hebrew culture, he is declared the Father's son; he has entered into the kingdom, his inheritance.

From this juncture in his life, Jesus preaches and prepares his disciples for the same experience. They too are called to be sons of the same Father, to realize their divine nature in conscious fashion, to inherit the kingdom. The inner transformation achieved by the intensification of the life force can now account for the superior morality of the disciples. Their whole attitude towards life and death, material possessions, ranking of prestige, endurance of pain and obstacles, ability to relate to others—all these aspects of the human personality are radically transmuted with the self-knowledge provided by the expansive life force. No longer living by faith, they have found the key to the kingdom: the awakening within of the divine life that stirs them to live an earthly life in union with divine awareness.

One can now understand that the experience of this transformation could hardly be put in words, let alone parables. The exact techniques of the preparatory initiations were always sheltered from the crowd. Thus the Gospels foretell of the good news of the kingdom but the keys are only given from teacher to disciple in readiness. Those preoccupied only with this world will never know that the mysterious knowledge of the kingdom is the self-transformation from their old Adam to the new. Born again into the spirit gives the ears to hear and the eyes to see the meaning of the parables and enables one to live the Sermon on the Mount.

YOGA AND THE JESUS PRAYER

One day in the middle of the nineteenth century, a young man attended religious services in a Russian Orthodox church. During the liturgy he heard the reading of Paul's letter to the Thessalonians. One text in particular struck his heart: "Pray without ceasing." His mind turned it over and over. Upon leaving the church he searched in his Bible to confirm what he had heard. He felt perplexed: How can one pray unceasingly? His urgency to satisfy this mandate forced him to search throughout the city for someone to explain the solution. Unsuccessful there, he wandered from city to village, village to monastery, monastery to city, always asking, always searching. Late one night he arrived at a monastery, having walked more than one hundred miles. He was welcomed in as a pilgrim. Immediately he implored anyone to explain the words of St. Paul, as he had done hundreds of times before. An old *startsi* (spiritual master) was called. Upon hearing of our pilgrim's plight, the old man crossed himself and smiled, "Thank God, my dear brother, for having revealed to you this unappeasable desire for unceasing interior prayer." Then he taught the pilgrim the centuries-old method known as The Jesus Prayer. The pilgrim searched no longer, but spent the rest of his life praying without ceasing.[1]

The story of the pilgrim highlights an ancient practice indigenous to Eastern Christianity. The methodical use of this prayer practice has been described from the Russian version of the *Philokalia*, a compendium of teachings and diaries from the Desert Fathers, the Greek Fathers, and theologians of Byzantine spirituality, from St. Anthony in the third century up to modern times. In these writings, a unique form of meditative prayer is explained. It has been customarily practiced by monks of Eastern Christianity throughout the centuries. St. Benedict of Nursia, the founder of Western monasticism, did not include this prayer method in his rule for monastic life, and thus it has not been known in the spiritual traditions of the West.[2] Only in the twentieth century has it been rediscovered for contemporary Western spirituality.

The method, known as The Jesus Prayer, consists of the simple, invariable formula: "Lord Jesus Christ, Son of God, have mercy upon me"[3] repeated again and again. Ideally, in learning the prayer the aspirant approaches a *geront* or *staretz* (titles for a spiritual advisor) for the proper instructions. The inspiration for the formula is grounded in the Bible and the meditations of the Greek Fathers. In 1351 an Orthodox Council officially approved the doctrinal justification for the prayer. This ecclesiastical achievement was largely due to the defending efforts of a fourteenth-century monk, Gregory Palamas of Athos, who later died as the Archbishop of Thessalonica in 1359. The written material required for the practice of the prayer was included in the *Philokalia*, "the love of spiritual beauty," codified in the eighteenth century.

The purpose of The Jesus Prayer is not merely ritualistic or devotional. Prayer had always been appreciated by the Christian East as a primary means for growth in self-knowledge. In The Jesus Prayer an interior transformation is also sought that leads to what the Greek Fathers called *theosis*, or the spiritualization of the personality.

Hesychasm, a spiritual tradition that dates back to the third century, uses the Jesus formula as one of its forms of inner prayer. The Hesychast monks (Hesychast means "the tranquil one") were especially noted for using this meditation as the chief means for their spiritual development. They combined prayer and meditation with breathing techniques as instructed by the monk Nicephorus the Solitary:

> You know, brother, how we breathe: we breathe the air in and out. On this is based the life of the body and on this depends its warmth. So sitting down in your cell, collect your

mind, lead it into the path of the breath along which the air enters in, constrain it to enter the heart together with the inhaled air, and keep it there. Keep it there, but do not leave it silent and idle; instead, give it the following prayer: "Lord Jesus Christ, Son of God, have mercy upon me." Let this be its constant occupation, never to be abandoned....These are the words of this blessed Father, uttered for the purpose of teaching the mind, under the influence of this natural method, to abandon its usual circling, captivity and dissipation and to return the attention to itself, and through such attention to reunite with itself, and in this way to become one with prayer and, together with prayer, to descend into the heart and to remain there forever.[4]

For a Christian practicing yoga this description is not merely similar to, but the same as, *japa* yoga. The constant remembrance of a sacred sound, *mantra*, is commonly referred to as *japa*. In yoga there is an ancient science of sound that permits the aspirant to use a series of syllables for the precise purpose of effecting an internal change in consciousness. The inherent power of the sacred sound, however, is not released in a mechanical way merely by its repetition. Preparation of the student, proper intonation of the sound, and the guidance of a qualified spiritual master make the practice effective. The *geront/staretz* served in the same capacity for the Hesychasts as does a master teacher in the yoga tradition—as the germinator of the seed-sound.

There is a certain naiveté in the Western attitude that believes one can choose an appropriate *mantra* for oneself. This thinking finds its logical extension in the idea that the laws of *japa* are a matter of taste or fashion. If one is not satisfied with a particular *mantra*, why not select another? To their eventual discouragement, such students will find that unless the laws of sacred sound are respected, their effects remain futile.

The Hesychast method involved the combination of breathing and mental concentration at a definite area of the body. The combination of these two factors immediately identifies the process as being similar to ancient yoga. The Hesychast practice of converging breath, concentration, and silent intonation at the heart region is a recognized yogic form of meditation. We have here an historical event in spirituality which links these two traditions. Whether these monks were informed yogis is not the issue. The descriptive facts of their method involve the laws of yoga whether the monks were cognizant of the tradition or not. Just how far back the monks started their method of prayer in this manner is difficult to trace, but the psycho-physical emphasis which facilitates the invocation of the name of Jesus corresponds to particular aspects of yoga and allows the ancient science to shed light upon this Christian method of prayer.

Yoga contributes to a greater understanding of this methodical prayer from its own laws of concentration. In the human body are definite gland and nerve centers, which, when interiorly focused upon by the mind, bring into play more subtle alterations of their energy. The stimulation of a particular area through breathing and concentration affects a gradual expansion of those positive qualities associated with the spiritual development of that area.

For example, in the yoga schema of spiritual development, when the heart region is properly stimulated, an increase in the aspirant's ability to love, to order one's emotions, is awakened. One becomes more sensitive affectively, especially to concerns of other people. A change of heart, a conversion, takes place. This change now influences one's vision of reality. One reverses selfishness. The personality unfolds with compassion, leading one into a new level of emotional integration. In yoga terminology, the stimulation of this heart center, the *anahad chakra*, purifies egocentrism. The same result is declared by the Hesychast monks when they speak of the purified heart being the abode of God. The method involves what the Fathers call a "natural" process. It is a retraction from the excitement of the senses, a silent intonation in rhythm with breathing, and an absorption of concentration upon the heart. Starting from the human situation of "fallen nature," as described by the monks, this technique attempts a return or restoration of one's nature to its original pure state. Sometimes accompanied by a feeling of warmth around the physical heart, the technique gradually leads to an awareness of one's higher self.

THE GOAL OF THE HESYCHAST: THEOSIS

The ultimate goal of the Hesychast method is the participation in divine consciousness. A process of conversion is undertaken in which attention is reversed from the external, created reality towards the inner spirit. In this way a return or ascent inward to a divine status or *theosis* takes place. The method has similarities with Patanjali's classical yoga system. The *Yoga Sutras*, like the Hesychast writings, designate a bodily and mental regime that gradually disposes one to greater self-knowledge. The coordinated disciplines bring a sense of mastery over human nature, spontaneously inducing a calmness of spirit that spreads throughout the body-mind complex. Amid that profound peace, the Hesychast and the yogi intuit their real nature.

As a result of poor living habits, modern people's constitution is weakened, their emotions embarrass them and their thinking is disoriented. Prone to grandiose illusions, addictions, and selfishness, their inflated egos obscure their real nature. Hesychasm purposes an orgasmic connection between body, mind, and spirit. By employing a psychosomatic method including posture, breathing, attitude, and concentration, human nature is rehabilitated into full spiritual actuality. For this conversion to *theosis*, the aspirant must struggle with two stages of inner development called *praxis* and *theoria*.

PRAXIS

For the Hesychast, *praxis* is similar to the moral code of yoga, the *yamas* and *niyamas*. The comparable asceticism aims at rectifying the dissipation of the senses and egotistical tendencies. Daily practice in bringing the senses and imagination under more rational direction permits fewer and fewer superfluous images and thoughts to distract concentration. In this way *enkrateia*, mastery of self, emerges. The Hesychasts insist that the experience of divine existence remains outside as long as one is unable to deal effectively with one's thoughts and passions. Patanjali likewise remarks that unless one controls the fluctuations of the body-mind complex, one's essential nature remains obscured: "Yoga is the control of the modifications of the mind. Then the seer is established in his own essential and fundamental nature."[5]

THEORIA

The second phase of inner development results from the virtuous efforts of *praxis*. The purifying struggle to reorder the bodily and mental faculties throws more light upon the nature of the world. The inner rectifying of the appetites, along with the restraint of egotism, effects a subjective cleansing, as it were, that allows one to be more objective. Reality is no longer a matter of mere personal preferences. The tempering of the senses produces a correcting effect upon the mental faculties. Self-deception about practical living wanes. One contemplates *(theoria)* the entire cosmos without imputing personal designs. Balance returns. The created world is seen with its relative merits. The purgative virtues, like yoga practices, effect discrimination. The Hesychast lives with what the yogi calls "meditation in action"—being in the world but not deceived about its nature.

According to St. Maximus, *praxis* purifies the intellect and body. The reintegration of the intellect and emotions leaves the power of intelligence keenly receptive. No longer dominated by the descent towards the material world, one's cleared intelligence now discerns the "divine wisdom invisibly contained in creatures."[6] Purgation has increased sensitivity, enabling one to recover the higher intuitive approach to reality. Instead of relying upon the limited framework of his rational faculty, he knows the external world in a superior way: from within.

Passing beyond the superficial knowledge of created things, one apprehends their eternal essences. With an immense expansion of discernment, states Philotheus of Sinai, "this purified heart becomes an interior sky with its own sun, moon, and stars, and circumscribes God, the Uncircumscribable, by the secret ascent of his vision."[7] Simultaneously with one's illumination, according to St. Macarius, the heart consciousness enlarges into a cosmic love: "the heart is aflame with love for every creature."[8] Saint Clement calls it *apatheia*, the cathartic control of the emotions that enables love to be strong and consistent.

Both Hesychasm and yoga describe an applied psychology for transforming human nature into its full actuality. The validity of either tradition lies not in authoritative declarations, however, but in the personal trial of the methods. In the daily testing through self-practice, the student can verify the methods' intrinsic worth. Both traditions also respect the various levels of the body-mind complex. While the terminology can often be interchanged in either methodology, the Hesychast descriptions retain a religious symbolism and are less detailed in their presentation of the psychological stages than those of the *Yoga Sutras*. The traditions agree from the start that the student's emphasis is on "enstasy," a re-entering into oneself, as opposed to "ecstasy," the energetic moving outward from oneself to things. Both understand that the preliminary ascetic practices lead to the interiorization of the mind's faculties, culminating in an expansion of consciousness.

Both traditions respect the fundamental life principle as it functions in the entire body-mind complex. Since breathing and the heart's action are indispensable for life, both methods incorporate these facts of animation. The intrinsic relationship between these two vital functions, however, is the basis for more than a matter of ordinary physiology. While breath gives life to the body, the Hesychast considers the body as "the temple of the spirit,"[9] the exact phrase the yogic sages use in their *Sri Vidya* tradition. The Hesychast accepts a dependence between breathing and the infusion of the life spirit or *pneuma*; air serves as a vehicle for vitality to enter into the body. From the spiritual point of view, the Hesychast sees *pneuma*, or the divine life breath, entering into one and making one a holy temple. Already manifesting God's image, one becomes and continues to be enlivened with God's life force through the action of breathing.

The physiological connection between breathing and heart action for physical well-being corresponds to a higher level of psychological and spiritual integration. The rhythm of breathing indicates the condition of one's health as well as one's spiritual vitality. The same life force, known as *prana* in yoga, promotes physical health as well as spiritual development. The Hesychast, like the yogi, recognizes the reciprocal communion between proper breathing and the lucidity of consciousness. According to St. Nicephorus the Solitary:

> You know that our breathing is the inhaling and exhaling of air. The organ which serves for this is the lungs which lie around the heart, so that the air passing through them thereby envelops the heart....Having collected your mind within you, lead it into the channel of breathing through which air reaches the heart, and together with this inhaled

> air, force your mind to descend into the heart and to remain
> there...the mind when it unites with the heart is filled with
> unspeakable joy and delight.[10]

The union of mind and heart in Hesychasm unexpectedly concurs with the meaning of yoga—the science of the unification of one's powers for one's full realization. The heart region is only one of several areas available to express various dimensions of one's personality. Although not described in the literature of the Hesychasts, these other centers of concentration which are associated with definite nerve ganglia throughout the body are fully elaborated in the yoga scriptures. Each of these seven major centers, called *chakras*, are responsible for characteristic personality development. The unfoldment of personality or spiritual restoration proceeds in either tradition from bodily disciplines and social virtues to inward concentration.

The early Christian communities symbolized their various practices in religious language that relied upon a close resemblance to the Hebrew culture and biblical terms. Although the Gospels were the Christians' constant resource for clarifying their aim, the natural explanation of becoming Christlike, the spiritual ascent, or *theosis*, can be equivalently interpreted from the holistic understanding provided by the yoga tradition. Both traditions assert the fundamental soundness of human nature. St. Simeon remarked that human deification is not a supernatural addition to mundane nature; *theosis* does not make one into a two-tiered being of nature plus supernature. Rather, the monk insisted, beneath ego and emotional cravings, which injure and blind one, lies a pure nature which "subsists fully, just as it was created."[11]

The Hesychasts do not speak of attaining something new but of recovering an inheritance already intrinsically possessed: the kingdom of heaven which lies within us. In order to discover this hidden kingdom, one must enter within and establish an interiorization of consciousness which is referred to as an "unknowing" or *agnosia*. Unknowing does not imply a condition of ignorance, but rather an unblemished awareness of reality without vested interests. One must leave behind any preference for the rational mode of uniting with the objects of knowledge. One must actively seek an inward retraction from egotistical conceptualizations. The ego's liking for conceptualizing reality, even God, forms the last temptation. From this pervasive tendency, the ego must be purified. As one interiorizes, the effort to objectify what the mind most wants to idealize—namely God—must also be abandoned.

The divine essence is not an idea. Neither is the experience of divine life. Unlike the cosmos, God's intelligibility can never qualify as an object of rational knowledge.

> The prayer of the heart must sweep away all imagination, both proper and improper...as wax melts in the fire, so does imagination disperse and disappear under the action of pure prayer through simple, imageless cleaving of the mind to God...since every thought enters the heart through imaging something sensory...so the light of the deity begins to illumine the mind when it is freed of everything and totally empty of form...as the Lord dwells not in temples built by human hands, neither does he dwell in any imaginings or mental concepts.[12]

Often Christians consider prayer and meditation as involving mental content. To elicit devotion, one must necessarily image the object of devotion. In the Hesychast tradition, however, the effort is eventually to eliminate any fluctuation of the mind. Ordinarily the mind focuses its attention in a limited way upon the object of devotion. The Hesychast instead desires to eliminate the focus of the mind, allowing for an openness so that the light of divine consciousness may fill the heart. In the late Middle Ages books on Christian enlightenment reiterated this same approach to spiritual development.

One finds in *The Book of Privy Counseling* such passages as:

> Reject all thoughts...see that nothing remains in your conscious mind save a naked intent stretching out toward God...leave your thought quite naked, your affection uninvolved and your self simply as you are...[13]

The Flemish monk, Jan van Ruysbroeck, in his *The Adornment of the Spiritual Marriage* remarked that:

Enlightened men are, with a free spirit, lifted above reason into a bare and imageless vision wherein lies the eternal indrawing summons of the divine unity; and with an imageless and bare understanding they reach the summit of their spirits.[14]

John of the Cross states that:

the soul must be emptied of all these imagined forms, figures and images, and it must remain in darkness in respect to these internal senses if it is to attain divine union.[15]

The student on the path must be alerted, therefore, to conceptual straps, less he misidentify the level of ideas about God with the experiential intuitive knowledge of God. In their writings, the monks Callistus and Ignatius note:

Since every thought enters the heart through imagining something sensory, so the light of the Deity begins to illuminate the mind when it is freed of everything and totally empty of form...[16]

In its supreme conclusion, the Hesychast path becomes strikingly similar to yoga. The positive unknowing or naked intellect is achieved through a process of stilling the mind. Dissociated from the slightest mental activity, subconscious or conscious, one breathes in undisturbed equanimity. An inner pacification that exceeds all descriptions reigns. In the undisturbed being of pure awareness without an object, the Hesychast and the yogi realize their absolute nature. Reversing the eternalization of consciousness, the vision of the divine becomes one with the vision of self. In perfect stillness, according to Evagrius, one has recovered one's original state.

MEDITATION:
AN INNER SCIENCE

Modern science is predicated upon its ability to verify its hypotheses. Verification is very important because it allows investigators to objectify their thoughts. Astronomers, for example, may not be sensibly aware that there is another planet in space, yet they hypothesize its existence on the data of the movements of the other heavenly bodies. Through their ingenuity, scientific investigators can occasionally predict the discovery of a new body.

An elementary textbook in chemistry may assert that water, H_2O, boils at 212°F at sea level. If someone had never ascertained that fact in personal experience, one would have to assume that the statement was true. Various textbooks would repeat that ordinary water reaches a boiling point when heat is applied to the intensity of 212°F. But how does anyone really know that the statement is true? How does one know it makes sense? Is the text correct? Does water boil only at this specific point? The textbook author may be a close friend, or may even possess a Nobel Prize, but are his or her assurances sufficient to make me feel secure in the knowledge that water boils at 212°F? Hardly. I want to know by experiencing the fact; otherwise doubts arise.

My mind is not satisfied with anything less than experience. Random and controlled experience is the raw material of scientific investigation. In other words, a scientific demonstration requires first-hand knowledge. Second-hand knowledge, textbook statements, words from an authority cannot guarantee the security of knowledge. Whether we are professionals who are striving to examine or comprehend a section of reality, or just someone who is interested in life in general, we prefer real facts to wishful hoping. Staying close to the facts of life helps us deal with the task of life. With facts, we have more possibilities for success in living than just hoping or praying that things will work out.

Nature is extravagant with her facts. So polymorphic is she in the display of her wares that various intelligible approaches are possible to obtain factual knowledge. Humans can be studied chemically, biologically, sociologically, psychologically, religiously, to name but a few. Each approach presupposes experiencing the facts but seeks more than their enumeration. Cataloging facts is not science. How and why facts are facts is what forges scientific knowledge about our universe and about ourselves.

People still refer to the universe as the "cosmos." The word is borrowed from ancient Greek philosophers, the first scientists of the West, and means "order." The implication is that human beings, as well as any portion of nature, are coherent realities wherein discernible facts constitute a unified, intelligible totality. The cosmos is an inter-related reality, accessible to human intelligence, which itself seeks to grasp its manifold order amidst the flux of life. The sciences, then, articulate the various connective orders lodged in the universe.

A human being as the subject of scientific investigation offers a twofold approach for study. First, one can be investigated by many of the mathematical-empirical based sciences like chemistry and physics, as well as studied by the social and biological sciences like anthropology and psychology. Secondly, as a living, self-conscious being who internalizes the facts of the cosmos and can affect cellular processes through awareness, the investigation of oneself as a conscious being is unique.

THE UNIQUE FIELD OF SCIENTIFIC STUDY: HUMAN CONSCIOUSNESS

One's interior world of consciousness is the field of scientific study called meditation. Meditation is the repeatable experiment in which the mind is both the investigator and its own laboratory. You, the investigator, in the practice of meditation, experiment directly with the source of your investigation and with its experiment—your own inner consciousness. This unique enterprise sets it apart from a mere psychological study of mental operations.

It may seem strange to investigate meditation as a science when for centuries temples, monasteries, and theological schools have espoused meditation as an essential part of their religious practices. Until the recent interest by university scientists in the nature and range of altered states of consciousness, prompted in part by biofeedback and mood-altering drugs, meditation has been associated with prayerful feelings and devotional attitudes. Yet today meditation is recognized in research circles as an important subject matter with therapeutic value, although the ancient science of yoga is seldom given the credit for meditation's contributions. Focusing upon the natural phenomena involved in meditation and leaving aside the religious associations, scientists are able to perform legitimate investigations. Consequently, the various religious methods of meditation can benefit from the serious research being conducted upon meditators.

FORMING THE MEDITATION HYPOTHESIS

In its search for secure knowledge, science attempts to establish its hypothesis by eliminating the variables and finding the constant factors in any experiment. Likewise, meditation follows a similar procedure. As a science, meditation hypothesizes that the investigator can discover, in an orderly and repeatable way, universal knowledge regarding the nature of human consciousness. Moreover, the methodological procedure—the introspective process—is capable of verification. The investigator or practitioner can discover and reproduce, by following standard procedures, sufficiently similar effects so that agreement on the results is confirmed. By submitting to principles of verification and predictability, meditation removes itself from the onus of a strictly private experience and allows for objective scrutiny.

For our presentation, meditation may be classified more as an applied science than as a theoretical science. The investigator/practitioner of meditation is not only studying thought patterns and mental operations just to know that they exist, but to detect the definite results upon his or her whole person discovering the latent potentials residing in human consciousness. Studying the mind is not on a par with studying nature in terms of physics, chemistry, or astronomy. The mind in its operations is on a different plane of reality than the atomic structures of matter, although it uses them in configuring its thought patterns.

Another comparison may aid here. When one turns from physics to biology, one is confronted with a different plane of reality. Biology, being the study of living organisms, is obviously a different field from theoretical physics. Since there is a radical difference in the subject matter—life's organic activities are more than the motion of atoms—one enacts a different methodology with appropriate concepts and laws that conform to the specific subject matter.

This clarification is necessary in order to avoid the temptation of judging all valid sciences as only subdivisions of physics or broad imitations thereof. The scientific enterprise is not, contrary to many scientists, a one-dimensional, quantitative way of knowing things. It must take into consideration the precise differences in the subject matter under study, which then call for a particular methodology. Reality is too diverse in its evidence to justify a single perspective to exhaust its riches. Genuine knowledge requires differing perspectives, approaches, and methodologies, and the investigator will employ different language terms to reflect his findings.

The study of human consciousness as living awareness uses the special methodology of introspection. Its procedures and results will thus differ from the quantitative expectations obtained in the physical sciences. Before outlining the meditation experiment in broad strokes, let us begin with some preliminary fact-finding at the common-sense level. Here ordinary introspection and reflection on everyday experiences will suffice for our purposes. Later, introspection will be used formally as a procedural tool throughout the experiment. The investigator will refine its application as s/he probes further into the experiment.

In a normal day, a scientist notices that his or her mind and body undergo various kinds of change. Endless thoughts and images occupy one's attention. Countless sensations and feelings affect the body. It is no different for the serious meditator. During a twenty-four hour period, neither the mind nor the body would seem to qualify as invariant constants eligible for experimentation. Both are changing their condition too randomly to allow for any consistency in results. Where does that leave the possibility of an experiment? For what else remains for the investigator/meditator to study but the body and mind? The question is whether the body-mind complex in its variable moods can demonstrate sufficient stability for prolonged study.

Granted that the body and the mind fluctuate incessantly throughout the day, everyone still feels and thinks that he or she is, nonetheless, in some vague fundamental way, the same individual who undergoes these recurring changes. A typical day may find one in different locales, weather conditions, and social surroundings, while thinking thoughts that have little to do with one's momentary environment. The range of varying episodes on any typical day are unpredictable as well as unlimited in their diversity. Yet the variety of intellectual and sensual experiences occur to the same person.

Like winds, our moods change and alter their strength spontaneously, yet always one senses continuity within oneself. Whether one experiences life as a series of fluid configurations, flowing and blurring into each other, or as a stack of contiguous snapshots, something abides that renders continuity to these episodes in spite of the unpredictable and often illogical occurrences that mix into each other. Life is less a quilt of experiences seamed together by the incidental threads of time, space, and location, than a continuing panorama that engages the self-same agent. While waking, dreaming and sleeping may comprise my apparent range of notable experiences, in between these traveled states my identity does not suffer annihilation. Somehow, something accounts for my sense of oneness throughout these experiences. Something about me sustains its existence without losing identity amidst the changes experienced. Without this perdurable, underlying reality upon which these mental and bodily changes take place, change itself would be impossible. Change cannot exist by and in itself; any change occurs or takes place in an existing reality. Thus, throughout all the changes in my physical, mental, and emotional makeup, the same "I" or sense of self-consciousness persists as the individual experiencer.

Given this brief review of the human experience of mood changes, let us now state the hypothesis that will be applied to the subject matter, namely, the fluctuating consciousness of the investigator. The hypothesis, then, is that the investigator will first proceed to investigate his or her own consciousness, noting its changes and, by applying throughout the investigation the appropriate method of introspection, will discover a stable order of reality that prevails universally among human beings. Secondly, the more the investigator performs this experiment, the more s/he will grasp the meaning of the experiment itself, that is, the nature of consciousness in its diverse conditions and states. This knowledge will provide, in addition to its content, increasing control over its use. The entire experimental process is called meditation. The practical use of the enterprise in daily life is called meditation-in-action.

TESTING THE HYPOTHESIS

The hypothesis is then carried out, or tested, by systematically setting up the conditions for the experiment in the recommended manner. A stationary posture is assumed, eyes are closed, and rhythmic diaphragmatic breathing commences. The prolonged coordination of this procedure gradually eliminates the disturbing sensual impressions from the environment and subdues the fluctuating images and concepts. The experimenter undergoes a systematic process by attentively directing, controlling, and observing the self-induced experiment. The relaxed stationary posture immobilizes the body and the willed rhythmic breathing settles the nervous system while calming the active imagination. The experimenter gradually focuses his or her inner attention in a designated manner that permits him/her to witness the entire quieting process. As the interiorization of this concentration lingers, the latent awareness of consciousness heightens. As the experiment is repeated daily, duplicating the sequence of steps, further disclosures in self-awareness occur as the experimenter refines the process. Repeated experiments stabilize the process while yielding more discernment and knowledge regarding the mind and its contents. The spontaneous increase in self-awareness proportionately increases the power of attention and control over the mind and its variables, the fluctuating contents.

One of the major breakthroughs in self-knowledge is through first-hand exposure that the experimenter/meditator now knows, namely, that one is not one's mental variables, that one is more than one's thoughts and feelings, however these may drive one's behavior, more than the customary conditions of consciousness that occupy one's normal hours. By investigating meditation, one investigates one's conscious life force; by investigating that force, one discovers the perdurable factor which not only gives continuity to life's experiences, but also remains intact through all personality changes. In the experiment of meditating, the investigator/meditator uncovers the basic constant: the individual field of awareness, the self-sustaining presence of one's consciousness.

This discovery is not a private, isolated event. Samplings of various other subject-meditators would concur with similar findings. The personal insight derived from the experiment expands into a universal knowledge about human nature. With continual exposures to the method, the experimenter eventually discovers that the dynamic constant of consciousness is the sole source that accounts for personality changes. The complex of values, attitudes, and behavior that distinguishes people in similar or different circumstances can now be traced to the dynamics of this constant in its interaction with life.

During the day, as well as in meditation, the mind processes various kinds of sense impressions and concepts. The mind assumes this content from the outside world or retrieves it from memory. Because of one's goals and tasks with life, it is helpful to build certain habits of interpreting life. The mind becomes fond of its mental habits—its paradigmatic ways of selecting, judging, and expressing. The problem is not so much that these habits are good or bad, practical or nonsensical. Rather these mental determinations may be preventing the meditator from increasing his or her understanding and enjoyment of life. A dependency grows for certain thought patterns or responses that constrain the mind to look at life from inflexible points of view. One hardly realizes how closely consciousness has aligned itself with its habitual stances. But persisting in meditation, one slowly recognizes that the fondness for these habits of perception and judgment may be useful but they are also definitely limiting.

MEDITATION AS A TRANSFORMATIVE SCIENCE

The experiment moves to another level of performance. Instead of merely cataloguing the thought patterns, meditation in its practical dimension promotes the ability to control the mind's wavering contents. The mental fluctuations and contents of the day, new and old, are the variables that need inner control in order to arrive at the subtler areas of consciousness. Control acts systemically in body, mind, and spirit. These mental modifications (*vrittis* in yoga philosophy) are appraised through the use of discernment (*viveka*). Through the act of meditation, an expansion of self-awareness occurs. By witnessing to the fluctuating contents of the mind, one discovers how easily one becomes enamored by the contents. A rebalancing can now ensue. The meditator can see where personal choices make one dependent upon one's limited mental outlook as the only way to appreciate life, rather than using the mental apparatus freely in the world. Without meditative awareness, the meditator was thus paving his or her own road of suffering (*klesas*).

Meditation, we now see, is the experimental science discovering and using consciousness for human freedom. Everything one does, feels, wishes, or imagines is possible because consciousness is the underlying, sustaining reality. Meditation is not a science of thinking; the reasoning realm is only one of the mind's discernible dimensions. As a process of interiorization, meditative investigation proceeds beyond the margins of thought into the regions of creative intuition, exploring the full range of consciousness.

As it is sometimes said in quantum physics, the observed is changed in the act of observing. So in meditation the meditator is unexpectedly changed in the act of observing. Clues emerge during daily experimentation which indicate that the meaning of the experiment is much more than the supposed, perfunctory investigation of mental states: increased tranquility, smoother coordination of body and mind, the waning of tension, more relaxed sleep, cardiac and blood pressure balance, among others. These recurring signs indicate that the experimenter is proceeding properly.

When the methodology, the interior experimentation of meditation, proceeds in an orderly manner, definite qualitative and quantitative results can be verified. In its method of investigation and in the results of its procedure, meditation is a special type of science whose goal or truth is both speculative information and especially a personal, transformative knowledge. In discovering the chemical contents of the human brain, for example, my behavior is unaffected; in discovering the nature of my mind through meditation, the power to change behavior is mine to express. Meditation is thus a practical science which transforms the investigator during the act of investigating. At the practical, everyday level of jostling with life, one learns through meditation that the foundation of happiness is laid within, and by consciously building upon it, a bridge is extended to intelligent living in the outside world.

THE DEVELOPMENT OF CHRISTIAN MEDITATION IN LIGHT OF YOGA

Among modern Christians there is a renewed interest in the meaning and direction of their spiritual life. At the forefront of this concern is the growing attraction for the practice of meditation and contemplation. Some believers, however, view these practices as highly novel—even offensive—and consider them a dangerous inroad by Eastern non-Christian influences or, at best, a temporary fad.

Surprising as it may seem to them, there is ample precedence for meditation and contemplation rooted in the Bible and eagerly developed from the inception of Christianity. This rich tradition espoused techniques and exercises that centered around achieving both inner quiet and the expansion of consciousness.

For centuries, then, the terms meditation, contemplation, and prayer have been variously commented upon in the writings of their practitioners. The range of interpretations accruing to these terms has often led to problems regarding their meaning and practical applicability. A clarification is needed.

A general survey of the inauguration of meditation, contemplation, and prayer within the growth of organized Christianity will trace some of the strands of meaning that became entangled and that produced the eventual confusion prevailing today. At the same time, the meaning of these terms as portrayed in representative textbooks on spirituality will be examined in comparison to the ancient yoga tradition.

THE DOUBLE TRADITION OF CHRISTIAN SPIRITUALITY

The event of Jesus Christ inspired in his followers a desire to pursue a life of ultimate significance. Amidst the Jewish and Roman cultures of the first three centuries, Christians gradually organized themselves into various groups or churches and adapted their master's teachings to their surroundings. These "followers of the way," as they were called, sought to engender in themselves the scriptural admonition, "You, therefore, are to be perfect, even as your heavenly father is perfect" (Matt. 5:48). Paul, the thirteenth apostle, mentions that Christians are "called to be saints" (Rom. 1:7, 8:28, 1Cor. 1:2), since "this is the will of God, your sanctification" (1 Thess. 4:3). While the exact adaptation of the Christian way of life was left to the individual churches, their overall direction was quite clear: Christians were to lead a life of evangelical integrity, that is, a life of poverty or detachment from worldly goods, chasteness, and obedience to the will of God.

The first two centuries of Christianity showed a twofold development in spirituality: institutional and monastic. After Pentecost the first bishops and priests were concerned primarily with the moral standards of their communities. These leaders wrote many letters that convey the direction, problems, and pressures of the time. The Epistle to Diognetus in the second century mentions,

> Christians do not differ from other men in country or
> language or peculiarity of life....For there are no towns set
> apart for them, nor language spoken by them alone, and
> there is no eccentricity in their manner of living....They
> inhabit the towns of the Greeks or the barbarians, as their lot

may be, and while following the customs of the country in which they are, whether in the matter of clothing or food or other habits, they lead an admirable sort of life which in the eyes of all men is to be taken to be a prodigy. Each one of them dwells in his country, everything as if they did not belong to the country...they are in the flesh, but they live not after the flesh. They obey the law but by their manner of life they are above the law.[1]

In their newfound approach to life, most Christians continued to live as ordinary citizens while maintaining a definite moral outlook on culture that was inoffensive (although somewhat baffling) to their Roman neighbors. For the next two centuries the Roman authorities became increasingly intolerant of the Christians and finally branded them atheists and enemies of the state. The terrible persecutions in the name of the Roman religion reached such atrocities, including martyrdom for hundreds of believers, that many Christians feared for their lives and abandoned their commitment to Christ rather than endure torture and martyrdom. The trials and oppressions finally ceased, so that the catacomb Christians could then practice their way unopposed, as a result of Constantine, the new Christian emperor, declaring Christianity to be the state religion in 313 A.D.

Ironically, in moving toward the future, the Christian hierarchy organized its communities by modeling them upon Roman law and politics. The biblical message was then shaped within this institutional framework.

Along with this institutional approach to spirituality, there existed another rarer phenomenon: the monastic ascetics. The Greek word *monos*, meaning "alone," is the root of the words "monk" and "monastery." These terms originally meant a person or place where one lived solitarily. Men and women responded to the challenge of living up to the scriptural injunctions with a fervor and intensity that awed most believers. From such ascetics' own writings and from eyewitness accounts of this period come descriptions of their austere daily regimes centered around prayer and meditation:

And when he [Anthony] had made an end of these things, he forthwith became a solitary monk, and he took no care for

anything whatsoever except his soul, and he began to train
himself in the habits of the strictest abstinence and self-
denial. And he took up his abode there in the desert by
himself and he shut himself in and he laid in a supply of
bread once every six months....He dwelt there in a place
which was like a cleft in the rocks, with the intention of
seeing no man and of being seen by none and he had his
abode there for very many years.[2]

Some of the monks lived on dry bread; some ate only once a
week. Some wore untanned skins of animals; some went
naked. Most monks slept little and lived in caves or outdoors
without shelter. Their poverty was absolute, and endurance
was their most cultivated virtue. The following advice of a
monk to a beginner was not too exaggerated from that
typically found: "Eat grass, wear grass, and sleep on grass, and
then thy heart will become like iron."[3]

The ascetics pursued a career that was incompatible with worldly values;
their concern was for the inner life of the spirit. The decadence of Roman
society included too many distractions that could impede their commitment.
The dangers of living during the Roman persecutions mentioned above, as
well as their profound desire for Christian perfection, no doubt influenced
their self-exile to the wilderness. The flight to the desert resulted in a diversity
of lifestyles. Those who chose to live alone were called anchorites or hermits,
while those choosing companionship in small groups were known as
cenobites, meaning "life in common."

The trek to the wilderness later captured the imaginations of Christians on
a fairly large scale. There were thousands of representatives in Egypt,
Palestine, Syria, and Asia Minor by the end of the fourth century.

And there were living in that mountain about seven
thousand brethren, and in the monastery in which the
blessed Pachomius himself lived there were living one
thousand three hundred brethren; and besides these there

were also other monasteries, each containing about three hundred, or two hundred, or one hundred monks, who lived together; and they all toiled with their hands and lived thereby, and with whatsoever they possessed which was superfluous for them they provided or fed the nunneries which were there.[4]

The three names most associated with the inauguration of desert life are Paul of Thebes, Anthony of Thebaid, and Pachomius.[5] It was Pachomius who later composed the first rule for cenobites to live in small communities. This was in approximately 320 A.D. Since the communities were more concerned about ritual and group prayer as well as the common life, they were less austere than their hermit neighbors.

Each day those whose week of service it was rose up and attended to their work; and others attended to the cooking, and others set out the tables and laid upon them bread and cheese, and vessels of vinegar and water. And there were some monks who went in to partake of food at the third hour of the day, and others at the sixth hour, and others at the ninth hour, and others in the evening, and others who ate once a day only; and there were some who ate only once a week; and according as each one of them knew the letter which had been laid upon him, so was his work. Some worked in the paradise (i.e., the orchard), and some in the gardens, and some in the blacksmith's shop, and some in the baker's shop, and some in the carpenter's shop, and some in the fuller's shop, and some wove baskets and mats of palm leaves, and one was a maker of nets, and one was a maker of sandals, and one was a scribe; now all these men as they were performing their work were repeating the Psalms and the Scriptures in order. And there were there large numbers of women who were nuns, and who closely followed this rule of life also.[6]

ORIGINS OF MEDITATION IN CHRISTIANITY

In their daily practices the Christian ascetics borrowed both techniques and attitudes from contemporary non-Christian sources. One can trace instances of Roman stoicism (Epictetus and Cicero) as well as Platonic and neoplatonic theory in their conceptions of the spiritual life. Similarly, the Christian theologians borrowed from the philosophical categories of Hellenic and Roman thought in explaining the theology of Christianity. One can easily read in St. Augustine, for example, the evidence of his use of Plato's dialogues. Even as late as the thirteenth century, Thomas Aquinas likewise espoused Aristotelian concepts within theological contexts. Thus it is not surprising that a careful examination of the philosophy of human nature implied by most of the desert monks in their writings shows a definite tendency for a neoplatonic interpretation.

The monks's writings reveal that their attempts to advance in the spiritual life also came by way of experimentation. Consequently, ascetic excesses are notable in the accounts of their lives. It is from these same individuals, however, that the practice of meditation evolved. This is not to say that Christ and the disciples or the ordinary believer did not meditate. There is sufficient scriptural evidence to the contrary. Even the Nag Hammadi scriptures seem to indicate that some Gnostic communities included meditation as an essential practice for Christian growth. Also, the Jewish Essene communities that practiced meditation were well-known to Jesus and his disciples. Institutional Christianity, however, did not emphasize the role of meditation. The ascetics and monks are the Christian exemplars who seriously involved themselves with meditation.

Since their lives were committed to the imitation of Christ, every one of their human acts, internal as well as external, was associated in their minds with this religious lifestyle. Their entire day was interpreted as a series of prayerful actions motivated by the intention of bringing themselves interiorly closer to the mind and heart of Jesus Christ. Within this perspective, meditation was practiced as a form of prayer—attunement with God. It was an indispensable pious exercise of the ascetics' daily life. Their commingling of prayer and meditation would not be unexpected, since their activities were always viewed from a religious standpoint. Even their breathing practices and bodily postures were put within a category of prayer. Although capable of being effectively engaged in without a religious context, the valuable techniques of meditation were nevertheless given a religious flavor and put at the service of the goal of prayer.

From the anchorite Evagrius of Pontus (345-399 A.D.), Christians received the first codified treatise on monastic prayer. Some of Evagrius' assertions on prayer show the juxtaposition of prayer and meditation. He mentions the traditional description that "prayer is an ascent of the intellect to God."[7] For Evagrius the notion of intellect, *nous*, had nothing to do with the rational mind. In his understanding of human consciousness, it is divided into two major levels. The rational or discursive level of consciousness depends upon the bodily senses to provide the data for thought. Exercising this part of consciousness did not lead one into the true realm of prayer. One had to supersede this level and arrive at the higher level that Evagrius called intellection. Reasoning, the customary operation of the mind during everyday activities, is one level, while the higher level, intellection, dispenses with ideas and sense impressions and is an immediate intuitive awareness. Because of this division of consciousness, he further mentions that "you cannot attain pure prayer while entangled in material things and agitated by constant cares. For prayer means the rejection of concepts."[8] Again he states that "prayer is the energy which accords with the dignity of the intellect; it is the intellect's true and highest activity."[9] And again, "Blessed is the intellect that is completely free from forms during prayer...and has acquired complete freedom from sensations during prayer."[10] For Evagrius, the intellect is a divine substance and thus capable of achieving a profound stillness, *hesychia*. The deepest realm of intellect places one into a divine awareness—the very goal of the Christian way. Evagrius considered this awareness the supreme mystical state, the deification of man that the monks speak of as the Christian's rightful destiny.

The yoga tradition of meditation coincides with this inner dynamism as described by Evagrius. Patanjali, the codifier of yoga (200 B.C.), who similarly indicates that when one is no longer bothered by sense impressions nor distracted by ideas or concepts, but has brought feelings, thoughts, and remembrances under control, then one becomes aware of his full identity. With similar insistence, yoga asserts that the primary practice for achieving this inner stilling of the mind, beyond forms, is meditation. Both Evagrius and

Patanjali recognize that the pursuit of ultimate significance, whether given a religious coloring or not, employs the same quieting of the mind's operations.

For Evagrius, when one lives out of this inner communion, one's entire life is sacramental; that is, any action is a sacred performance, motivated from this highest state of divine awareness. In an ancient yogic text, the *Bhagavad Gita*, Krishna similarly tells his student, Arjuna, that when actions are performed from an attitude of divine service, they become acts of worship.

In carefully assessing the inner dynamics of these two traditions, a virtual identity emerges. The depiction of the process of stillness differs only by the pious symbols and historical context within which it is expressed.

As the centuries passed, variations of prayer and meditation enriched monastic spirituality. The most notable emphasis came in the acceptance of the interior process called The Jesus Prayer, discussed in Chapter 5. As early as the fourth century, Abbot Makarios of Egypt answered an aspirant's question about how to pray by telling him to say, "Lord, save me."[11] It is quite likely that the Jesus Prayer developed from the Kyrie eleison, "Lord have mercy," found constantly in the Christian liturgy. Although other monks used abbreviations of the prayer such as "Jesus have mercy," or "Christ have mercy," the precise formula of the Jesus Prayer—"Lord Jesus Christ, son of God, have mercy upon me"—achieved its final form during the sixth century when an Egyptian hermit, Abba Philomon, explicitly used it in this manner.[12] So is it practiced to the present day.

THE CONSOLIDATION OF MONASTICISM

Differences in emphasis and cultural development between Roman and Byzantine Christianity were evident in their approaches to spirituality and hence to meditation. Western Christianity attempted to develop the implications of the Gospels within a Roman organizational framework. Civil and religious spheres grew closer together during the Middle Ages in feudal Europe and religious practices became more regulated by canon law and Church authority. It is true that monasteries still retained their individual autonomy, but monastic observances were becoming increasingly standardized. It became mandatory for the monks to assemble for the solemn chanting of prayers and scripture called the Divine Office. This praying in common at set hours daily assumed the central act of the monastic life.

Meanwhile, the hermetic tradition survived in the West, although not to the vast extent that it did in the Middle East. This Western tradition, too, began to change after the large monasteries erected vaults beneath their ground floors for the local hermits. These rooms or cells adjoined one another, enabling their inhabitants to communicate discretely. Thus the cenobite life slowly eclipsed the desert ideal of strict isolation. Living within a monastery became the norm for those seeking the higher way. This legislative development was brought about by St. Benedict of Nursia (480-547 A.D.), the founder of Monte Cassino Abbey in Italy. His rule for regulating the monastic schedule became the prototype for the various monasteries that eventually became a federation in the tenth century. No doubt meditation, especially the Hesychast form was known to the monks but its explicit endorsement is nowhere mentioned in Benedict's rule.

Byzantine Christianity was not as structured as the Roman Church, and its monks followed primarily the rules of St. Pachomius and St. Basil, which were less regimented. Anchorites presented a problem; many wandering hermits were considered an embarrassment to the monasteries and towns and were eventually accused of disturbing society. In response to these complaints, Emperor Justinian issued decrees in the sixth century that compelled eremetical monks to live in monasteries.

Still, there was an admiration for those monks who felt called to the solitary life. The problem was handled in a unique way. As a monk progressed in the monastic life, he could eventually arrive at sufficient maturity where he would decide to leave the cloister and retire to the desert. In this way he was still connected to the monastery but had sufficient liberty to satisfy his desire for a closer union with God in solitude. This development in Eastern monastic spirituality is described in the Ladder of Paradise by St. John Climacus, who was himself a hermit who had started out as a cenobite. Thus, the principal reason that the eremetical tradition never died out in the East was the profound conviction that it was the crowning path of spirituality.

THE FLOURISHING OF THE SPIRITUAL LIFE

A similar respect for the monastic vocation was preserved in the West. According to Pourrat in his history of Christian spirituality, "from the sixth century, and during the great part of the Middle Ages, spirituality in the West is found almost exclusively in the monastic rules, which were drawn up in great numbers."[13] Nevertheless, following a rule did not constrain the most flourishing experimental period in the Western history of Christian spirituality. For almost a thousand years, the approaches of saints and mystics to Christian sanctity were exceedingly diverse as illustrated by the variety of monasteries, convents, and schools of spirituality that emerged in Europe.

The Middle Ages displayed a novel creativity as well as a reliance upon traditional texts of the desert ascetics in regard to the theoretical details of meditative states of consciousness. Many monasteries and schools of spirituality accepted as a unique guide the revered writings of Dionysius the Areopagite. Dionysius understood the spiritual journey primarily as a meditative process leading to a supra-rational knowledge of God in which, without the mediation of sense images and concepts, one knows immediately and directly. This direct vision at first obscures the mind with its dazzling light, for the mind simply can not comprehend the abundance of truth. The intensity of this vision, in turn, causes an obscuring darkness to envelop reason and the senses. Like an owl facing the brilliance of the sun, the untrained mind is unable to grasp the reality. Nevertheless, Dionysius understood this darkness as the presence of God.

As one continues to meditate and enter more fully into the silence of this darkness, one's consciousness undergoes a conditioning process that enables the *nous* to withstand the force of the transcendental experience—yoga refers to this physical and psychological conditioning as *adhikara*, the ability to hold the power—that initially produced the darkness.

In one of his principle works called *De Mystica Theologia* (The Hidden Knowledge of God), Dionysius counsels:

> In the earnest exercise of mystical contemplation, you leave
> the senses and the operations of reason and all things that
> the senses of reason can perceive, to the end that you raise

> yourself by this unknowing to union with Him who is above all being and all knowledge; that is, to raise yourself by absolute detachment from yourself and all things, stripped of everything and free from every hindrance to that stream of divine brightness coming forth from this inner obscurity.[14]

The texts of Dionysius were attributed to Denis, traditionally held to be the bishop of Paris and the companion of St. Paul. Thus great reverential deference was paid to his words. Ironically, these texts were later proven to belong to the sixth century, most likely written by an anonymous monk in Syria. They were finally translated into Latin, entering the West officially in 877 A.D.

Many saints and theologians found the Dionysian texts a reputable map for their spiritual journey. The medieval theologians and monastic founders assimilated the Dionysian doctrine on meditation into their own writings. Scotus Erigena, the Victorines, Albertus Magnus, Bonaventure, Thomas Aquinas, Meister Eckhart, Henry Suso, and many other authors cite the Syrian texts as a spiritual authority.

Echoes of Hesychasm found its way into many Western writings of this time. Richard of St. Victor (died 1173) describes the highest state of spirit as "the hidden place of inner quietness, the sanctuary of the highest tranquility."[15] Edmund Rich of Canterbury (1180-1240) speaks of first contemplating one's wondrous nature and God's beneficence. He tells the student, after being awed by the goodness and beauty of life itself, to "put every corporal image outside your heart, and let your naked intention fly up above all human reasoning."[16] The anchoress Lady Julian of Norwich (1343-1413) says, "The soul is united to God when she is truly pacified in herself."[17] St. Catherine of Sienna (1347-1380) speaks of the peace achieved through meditation: "The state of the soul is then a feeling of such utter peace and tranquility that it seems to her that her heart and her bodily being and all both within and without is immersed in an ocean of utmost peace."[18] The anonymous fourteenth century English author of the well-known works The Cloud of Unknowing and The Book of Privy Counseling makes use of a phrase similar to the "naked intention" used earlier by Rich:

By pursuing your meditation to the farthest reaches and ultimate frontiers of thought, you will find yourself in the end, on the essential ground of being with the naked perception and blind awareness of your own being....Leave the awareness of your being unclothed of all thoughts about its attributes, and your mind quite empty of all particular details....This blind awareness...will far surpass the value of any particular thought, no matter how sublime.[19]

These works reiterate the meditational tradition that carried its influence even into the stirrings of the modern ages with the writings of John of the Cross and Teresa of Avila.

THE REGIMENTATION OF THE SPIRITUAL LIFE

After the sixteenth century, the brilliant tapestry of medieval spirituality shrank to a cloth of just a few colors. An exciting new secular era broke upon the unprepared Christian West. The mixture of the Black Plague, the discovery of the New World, the Galilean embarrassment, and the mounting tensions between church and state produced such civil and religious upheavals that the Christian leaders enforced a siege mentality. Western Christianity divided itself into separate reform groups as a religious and political response to the decadent excesses pervading the institutional church. Allegiance to the various churches became strictly defined with militant overtones. The creative liberty enjoyed by men and women in exploring the steps to their spiritual destiny became more and more curtailed. Methods and exercises were closely scrutinized and increasingly standardized. For the supposed protection of Christians, a suppressive atmosphere was legislated throughout Europe. Spiritual orthodoxy lost its flexibility and became restricted to fixed methods that required official approval.

In an effort to defend itself against other, erroneous types of spirituality, Catholics and Protestants set up carefully monitored instructions on the unfoldment of the spiritual life along with its limitations and dangers. The aspirants were obliged to follow certain orthodox methods. Within this strict milieu, experimentation and unfamiliar methods, however valid, brought suspicion and censure upon the innovators.

The sixteenth century also saw a general reformation by Roman Christianity taking place during the forty-five year period of the Council of Trent. From this point on, no new monastic orders were permitted to be instituted. Adjusting to the signs of these times, religious communities no longer were to be involved in the eremetical life. The only exceptions made were for the monastic orders already in existence. Instead, new congregations were formed for the purpose of active engagement in the needs and growth of society. One of the most important of these was the Society of Jesus, also called the Jesuits, founded by St. Ignatius of Loyola.

The impact of Roman Christianity's attitude towards the modern era changed the emphasis in practices of meditation. Pourrat remarks that "in the days of St. Ignatius' conversion, meditation had become methodized, prayer regulated and the whole spiritual life organized and its various exercises so coordinated as to create a real system of moral reformation."[20] Up to this time, the goal of meditation was to achieve Christ-consciousness. Now the goal emphasized a moral conversion to the life of Jesus. To illustrate how this transformation was to take place, let us examine one of the most popular methods of meditation for these new religious communities—the Spiritual Exercises of St. Ignatius.

The exercises are divided into four weeks of meditations that are generally guided by a retreat director. The first week is designed to help aspirants purify their souls and put their lives in order; the aim of the second week is to lead souls to a greater knowledge of and love for Jesus Christ; the third week is devoted to freeing the will from the psychological obstacles that stand in the way of a decision to follow Christ; and the fourth week is intended to purify the heart in the highest degree from false attachments to creatures, goods, or worldly ambition and honor.

For those who are unable to follow the four-week regime, an intensive eight-day retreat condensing the entire method can be used. Whichever length is taken, there is no omission of the following four key meditation steps:

1. The aspirant begins with a preparatory prayer in which s/he begs that all intentions and actions be solely directed to the service and honor of the Divine Majesty.

2. One conjures in the imagination the composition of place. If the object of meditation is a biblical scene, the appropriate images relating to that scene are stirred up in order to dwell upon it. Should the object of meditation be sin, for example, one may fantasize ugly scenes in order to provoke a horror for sin. After sufficient time, one petitions God for the special graces to be obtained by this meditative step.

3. The central portion of the meditation involves the exercise of the various faculties of the soul—the memory, the intellect, and the will. The memory vividly portrays the material or object to be discursively meditated upon. The intellect then reflects upon the object and discerns what practical applications to one's daily life may be drawn from this consideration. The will deliberately arouses feelings of devotion about these discursive truths or awakens a feeling of the presence of God. With the affections amplified, one's will should now decide on and carry out a practical resolution inspired by the aforesaid process.

4. One should conclude meditation with devout colloquies with the saints or the Godhead, and survey this entire meditative process noting its imperfections and how to improve it.

The entire period for this method may last twenty minutes or as long as an hour, depending upon one's fervor or available moments.[21]

The Ignatian method of meditation and other similar methods carefully regulated one's moral transformation. Instead of using the more spontaneous and creative writings of the Desert Fathers and the saints of the Middle Ages, standard manuals that divided and subdivided the stages of the interior life were mandatory for clerical aspirants. They gave a finality to the terms and meaning of spiritual progress. The practical impact of these writings left the impression that they were the safe methods available by which to achieve perfection. Consequently, many of the older writings were neglected for the sake of producing a unified outlook on the constitution of official spirituality.

This organized approach of approved instructions for religious personnel has come down into the twentieth century.

THE REDUCTION OF SPIRITUALITY TO MORAL TERMS

Despite such rigid interpretations of meditation, the monastic traditions found in both Eastern and Western Christianity retained a similar appreciation regarding the dynamics of meditation. Yet each group produced practitioners whose writings show an originality in their contributions to the inner life. These writings obviously reflected both their own cultural images and their concerns for providing proper guidance, since they were aware that their texts would be utilized as instruction guides for aspirants. While the theories of meditation, contemplation, and prayer were assigned to the same ambit of spiritual progress, the words used to describe one's experience of each were often interchanged. The need for precision in language did not seem to be an issue. In fact, the higher states of meditation are exceedingly difficult to describe in any graphic manner since the experience is devoid of images and concepts. The practitioners often resorted to poetic description or made use of symbols that only hinted at these transcendental moments. Use of a wide leeway in choice of terms was often the case.

After the Reformation, however, this necessary poetic license was radically reduced to an orthodoxy in line with the defensive posture of the church authorities. The composition of spiritual writings now insured a standard vocabulary and a fixing of the terms. An unforeseen problem immediately occurred in the official acceptance of a rather fluid association between prayer, meditation, and contemplation. In attempting to elucidate these experiences with distinct categories of meaning, theologians increased the confusion of terms by misdefining them!

In order to illustrate this misunderstanding, two representative spiritual manuals explaining meditation and contemplation have been selected from the many volumes written within the Christian tradition. One manual by Reverend A. Tanquerey entitled *The Spiritual Life* has been used extensively in monasteries and convents in America and Europe. It states:

The terms meditation and mental prayer are often interchanged. When differentiated, the former is applied to that form of mental prayer wherein considerations and reasonings predominate and which, owing to this, is called discursive meditation.[22]

A more contemporary manual, *The Theology of Christian Perfection*, written by two monks, states that:

Discursive meditation can be defined as a reasoned application of the mind to some supernatural truth in order to penetrate its meaning, love it and carry it into practice with the assistance of grace. The distinguishing note of meditation is that it is a reasoned or discursive type of prayer, and therefore attention is absolutely indispensable. As soon as one ceases to reason or discourse, he ceases to meditate. He may have given way to distraction, deliberately turned his mind to something else, passed on to affective prayer or contemplation, but without discursus there is no meditation.[23]

Both manuals consider meditation as an exercise of prayer; indeed, a lower form of prayer suitable only for beginners on the spiritual path. Whatever method of discursive meditation or mental prayer one selected was viewed as only a temporary means to spiritual progress. Beginners were cautioned that these meditational methods could get in the way of progress. The road to perfection demanded that one eventually dispense with meditation.

The manuals portray contemplation as a more advanced stage than meditation. Contemplation is seen as a supernatural gift from God, rendered gratuitously to the aspirant. The aspirant has no claim upon it, nor can one induce it by one's own efforts. Like meditation, it is also understood as a form of prayer:

Contemplation is an operation in which one experiences the happy blending of the cognitive and the affective powers in an activity which is at once intuitive and delightful.[24]

> Contemplation is produced through the operation of the gifts of the Holy Spirit...consequently one cannot contemplate mystically whenever he wishes.[25]

The manuals are careful to insist that since the object of contemplation is the Godhead, the human faculties by themselves are incapable of apprehending such a profound object. Some condescension on the part of God must be involved if mortals are to contemplate him. God, in his infinite mercy, must bestow or infuse upon the human faculties the added capacity to reach out, as it were, to an object that normally exceeds the mind's field of operation. In this way, the divine bestowal of grace makes the act of infused contemplation not a natural act of human cognition, but a supernatural act, an act that is above and beyond the innate range of human endeavor. Contemplation may be performed only on God's terms. The contemplative act of awareness remains irreproachably outside of a human being's finest capacities.

This is a strange paradox. The spiritual manuals were meant to guide aspirants to the highest states of sanctity. Yet their complexity of prolix terms and complicated distinctions make their efficacy as guides practically nil. The simple yet profound tools of meditation and contemplation that guided the saints were thus reduced to beginner's practices or unattainable gifts.

THE ECLIPSE OF THE MYSTICAL LIFE

During the modern period, the emphasis of spiritual direction by many theologians, priests, and ministers turned from emphasizing a contemplative spirituality to forging a morally good and prayerful character in believers. The goal of institutional spirituality was to protect people from sin and prepare them in this "vale of tears" for heaven. The purpose of monastic living, which had long been to achieve stillness and union with God in meditation, became over-shadowed by church law's mandates for orthodoxy.

The spiritual manuals emphasized an orthodoxy derived from a constrained atmosphere. The spiritual quest emphasized acquiring Christian virtues, and as a result of this priority, one's use of prayer, meditation, and contemplation was put almost exclusively at the service of cultivating a moral individual rather than expanding consciousness into the wonder of the spirit. One cannot help but ask a persistent question: What has happened to the profound experiences and the high states of consciousness reported in the lives of the hermits and mystics?

The direction of the spiritual life as legislated by the Council of Trent and the popularity of the reformist's book, *Pia Desideria,* had its effects both on monastic living and on the lives of ordinary Christians: standardized practices were decreed; monastic life became complicated (it was not the simple life of the ancient tradition any longer); and the methods of meditation of the ancients were practiced less and less while their place was filled with community activities. Added to the Divine Office were other duties such as daily liturgy and works of charity that supported the moral development of the virtues. The amount of time spent in meditation and contemplation was enormously reduced. This consequently produced a very different atmosphere in monastic living. The achievements of the Desert Fathers and the medieval mystics were seen to be such a distant goal that they were classified, even in spiritual texts, as a rare grace that most people could never practically hope to obtain.

CONTEMPORARY MEDITATION

Among all the events that have occurred in our disruptive century, there are two that have had very significant consequences upon the development of the practice of meditation. The first event occurred in 1962 when the largest church in Western Christianity, Roman Catholicism, underwent a revolution in self-examination. This event was called the Second Vatican Council. For three consecutive years in Rome, clerical representatives from Catholic dioceses of the world met, discussed, and debated the Church's position vis-a-vis the modern world and its problems of meaningful survival. The Council took as its watchword *aggiornamento*—an updating, a deliberate admission that the Church was falling behind the times and needed drastic revisions in order to become relevant to contemporary society. For many of the professionally religious, these new changes came too late. In the after effect, thousands of religious men and women resigned from monasteries, convents, and religious houses to join the ranks of the laity.

The second event occurred shortly thereafter. Spiritual teachers from the Eastern hemisphere traveled to the West and exposed thousands of people to the Eastern traditions of meditation. Unknown to most Christians, these traditions show a remarkable resemblance in methodology and content to the ancient Christian tradition of meditation.

A strange reversal resulted from this combination of events. As more and more Christians began to accept the experiential truth of these practices, the laity took the lead in incorporating meditation into their daily lives. The surprising result is that institutional monasteries have begun to follow suit. In some of these groups one can find a return to the early Christian meditative texts that were so prevalent during the first fifteen hundred years of Christianity's existence, and that had been ignored for so long.

MEDITATION IN YOGA: A CLARIFYING COMPARISON

For contemporary Christians who may be interested in meditation, it is advantageous to compare the yoga tradition of meditation with the customary theological meanings of meditation and contemplation for the sake of avoiding misunderstandings in their renewed roles in the spiritual life. The term meditation possesses an entirely different meaning and use in yogic writings than in the post-reformational manuals. It is not employed in any religious context, nor does it presuppose any particular theological framework. Similar to the Christian manuals, however, yoga meditation directs its techniques to a practical goal, but instead of concentrating on the moral growth of the individuals, (which is only a part of the preparation for meditation), yoga meditation strives to transform individuals by expanding their self-awareness. This expansion is not an increase nor a refinement of ideas or images but a systematic inner experiencing of richer levels of the reality of one's nature.

In the *Sutras*, Patanjali classifies the ancient experiential tradition of yoga meditation as both a superconscious state of being and as a process that leads to that state. He defines the process as "the uninterrupted flow of the mind towards an inner object."[26] The goal of the meditator is nothing less than the full disclosure of one's profound nature.

In Patanjali's analysis of human consciousness, there is a distinction between the non-imaginative and non-conceptual state of consciousness and the expression of this same consciousness in its conjunction with the human body. Consciousness ordinarily utilizes the body as its instrument during the combined psycho-physical acts of sensation, imagination, and conceptualizations that mediate the customary knowledge of the external world. The physical body is the organic correlate to the mental operations of consciousness that are collectively referred to as the *antahkarana*. At this juncture, the psychosomatic structure found in the *Sutras* would be amenable to the Christian manuals' outline of the body-mind complex. Yet there is a major difference between the manuals and the *Sutras*. The manuals insist that the mind or consciousness in itself is inactive or passive, that it cannot perform cognition without the instrumentality of the mental faculties being stimulated by the input from the external world. By contrast, the *Sutras* assert that the soul's consciousness subsists in its operation, that it never ceases to be in a state of awareness. While the soul may utilize the *antahkarana*, or the mental faculties, in conjunction with the sense organs, there is, nevertheless, no essential dependence upon them. In fact, through the continual practice of yogic meditation, the practitioner gradually experiences a differentiation in awareness between the discursive contents of his mind and his immanent act of awareness. In other words, there is a dawning awareness: "I am not my thoughts; I am the thinker not the thoughts." This discovery is comparable to Evagrius' view of the totality of human consciousness mentioned earlier.

In the modern Christian methods of meditation, one remains within the field of one's mental faculties and dwells upon images and ideas. Obviously these cognitive truths could very well inspire their practical fulfillment in daily life. But, according to the *Sutras*, the highest state of consciousness requires the meditator to expand awareness beyond the operation of the discursive mind, for whatever is presented discursively is always rooted in the sensory data from which it arose. To this extent, the discursive mind cannot help but grasp its knowable objects in a conditioned, finite, incomplete fashion. Even to speak of infused contemplation as the divine bestowal of ideas or truths does not allow one to exceed the natural, internal limitations of the mind's faculties.

If there is any dependency upon the mental faculties, however subtle, the act of meditation or contemplation remains subject to the imaginative and discursive fields of finite consciousness. Even if one could still the movement of mind at the discursive level, one would then have to reckon with the surging forth of the subconscious field of memories. In either case, concepts and memory images occupy the mind's attention, and the transcendental state of mystic union remains only a distant yearning.

A question arises: Do the traditional theological manuals chart the processes of meditation and contemplation as these were actually performed by Christian mystics? Or, is the theoretical scrutiny of the mystics' writings restructured into the manual form to fit with certain theological presuppositions?

A certain dualism is preserved and sustained in the way the manuals treat the relationship between the meditator and the meditator's goal throughout this spiritual evolution to the highest state of contemplation. Yet the mystics themselves contradict this theological presupposition. St. Teresa speaks of "an utter transformation in God." A medieval work called *Theologia Germanica* asks the question: "What is it to be a partaker of the Divine Nature, or a God-like man? He who is imbued with the Eternal or Divine Light and inflamed or consumed with Eternal or Divine Love, he is a deified man and a partaker of the Divine nature."[27] That the notion of "deification" is not an innovative term spun out of the hallucinations of some obscure but overzealous believer is verified in similar works throughout the centuries. The Church Father St. Athanasius remarks in speaking of the purpose of the Incarnation of the Word of God, "He became man that we might become God."[28] In the words of Meister Eckhart, "If I am to know God directly, I must become completely He and He I, so that this He and this I become and are one I."[29] A medieval mystic, Richard of St. Victor, speaks of deification: when the soul "is plunged in the fire of divine love, like iron, it first loses its blackness, and then growing to white heat, it becomes like unto the fire itself. And lastly, it grows liquid, and losing its nature is transmuted into an utterly different quality of being."[30]

From this brief survey of mystics, the description of the ultimate attainment by those who had reached it reveals less of a duality than a unitive state of being. These meditative seekers of the transcendent absolute describe the consummation of their quest in the language of a transforming union so far above the imagination of orthodox believers as to scandalize them. While their metaphors and analogies may differ according to their cultural background, temperaments, and tastes, an insistence runs through their writings of one's latent absoluteness, expressed in a multitude of symbols. This absoluteness transcends the discursive faculties, expanding the meditator's awareness into the pure, unstructured experience of infinite consciousness. Meditation and union with reality become one. As the Christian mystic Ruysbroeck said,

> Thus do we grow and, carried above ourselves, above reason, into the very heart of love, there do we feed according to the spirit; and taking flight for the Godhead by naked love, we go to the encounter of the Bridegroom, to the encounter of His Spirit, which is His love; and thus we are brought forth by God, out of our selfhood, into the immersion of love, in which we possess blessedness and are one with God.[31]

The poetic quality of his language is distilled by the more abstract and metaphysical terminology of Patanjali, where the goal of meditation is described as total self-realization. The yogic meditator, like the Christian meditator, expands to the inexhaustible state of infinite knowledge; one's soul or individual consciousness is engulfed by the absolute cosmic consciousness. Certainly, in the beginning, a similar dualism appears between the yogic meditator and his or her experience of meditating. As the meditator continues the inner practices, a dawning intuition reveals that mind and body, spirit and matter, inner reality and outer reality are only apparently separated. What has started out as obviously dual at the sense and mental levels, recedes into an unparalleled unity at the absolute state of blissful or blessed awareness.

If one may compare the East and West as we have done, then certain revisions may be advanced. The Christian manuals' treatment of meditation is improperly limited. The imagination and discursive activity of mental prayer by its own standards retains the practitioner within the sensory and conceptual field of awareness. Reaching God or a transcendental state is prevented by the very instructions given for the activity. Christian contemplation being akin to intuition—although as the manuals understand it, still using the mental faculties—likewise keeps the aspirant from any transcendental experience. Yet the evidence of authentic transcendental states in the Christian tradition can be found by examining the lives and texts of the mystics' writings themselves. In comparison, the manuals measure their acceptable interpretation of these writings by certain psychological and theological criteria, which do not seem to do full justice to the evidence.

In view of our comparison, certain clarifications can now be made. Strictly speaking, meditation is not prayer. Prayer engages the mind, whether one prays to or for someone, in reference to its understanding of God. It, like contemplation, uses images and thoughts. Contemplation may be defined as a savoring reflection upon a particular idea or external object. Since prayer and contemplation are discursive activities, the practitioner would benefit within the borders of those activities. Meditation, however, is essentially a non-discursive, inward journey of the mind to expand beyond the discursive dimension and discover all the levels comprising the spirit in order to be in perfect union with them. This discovery of meditation leads to complete self-realization, a union with the divine.

In concluding, if one accepts Underhill's definition of mysticism as "the art of union with Reality,"[32] then an unexpected convergence arises, for this definition equally spells out the meaning of yoga.

THE MEANING OF REVELATION

Sacred scriptures, if they have meaning, must reveal that meaning in our lives today. To read the Torah for inspiration indicates that the reader assumes the life and law of Moses have value for modern living. Likewise, for a Christian to read a letter of St. Paul assumes that the contents pertain in some way to the twentieth century as well as to the first.

People revere sacred scriptures not just for their historical significance, but especially for their personal significance. The value of scriptures is their universal import. They can affect people in different cultures at varying periods of history. Not every passage in scripture, however, necessarily inspires in the same way. Consequently, the challenge of interpretation accompanies the endeavor to understand revelation.

This chapter will explore the problem of interpreting revelation by first discussing the composition of scripture, and second, how to approach interpretation as a tool for understanding scripture. To aid this approach, the contribution of yoga is explained.

THE NATURE OF REVELATION AND ITS LEVELS OF MEANING

One speaks of the Bible or any scripture as a revelation. Truth has been exposed. These revealed truths have such a stature because they are meant to guide people in understanding the ultimate meaning of life. To communicate universal truths throughout centuries, in varying cultures, would require a dexterity of expression. The versatility of genre often found in scripture would indicate that transcendental truths can, and indeed must, have more than a single articulation. The Jewish and Christian scriptures are typical examples.

As a written account of centuries of accumulated revelation, the Bible is more like a library in many volumes than a single work. As a compilation of legends, parables, aphorisms, songs, sagas, poetry, sermons, legislation, historical decrees, epics, liturgical rules, quotations, and myths, these writings offer a wide mixture of literary genre to say the least.

The various types of writings indicate different authors and editors, most of whom have remained anonymous. The biblical languages resemble everyday graphic changeable nature and do not easily lend themselves to abstract concepts. More concrete than abstract, more fluid than fixed, more poetical than scientific, these ancient languages possess those qualities of imagery that writers delight in—enigmas, puns, slang, irony, satire, and play on words. Their reverence for holy writ did not prevent them from taking advantage of every tool and every occasion.

The story of Samson in the Book of Judges illustrates a typical episode that has become an exaggerated legend. Samson's exploits are really war stories suitable for stirring the morale of the Israelites in their battles with the Philistines. The famous scene where Samson survives an attack of a thousand men by using the jawbone of an ass for his weapon and later throwing it away is an amusing tale. It relies upon the reader's appreciation of puns. The name of the hill upon which this incredible victory took place was called Leki, which means "jawbone." When reading the story in Judges 15:9–17 one also must remember that the word "hill" in Hebrew is pronounced in the same way as the word for "to throw away."

The exploits of the great King David are likewise immodestly embellished. In 1 Samuel 17:4–54 we read the story of how young David killed the giant

Goliath with a smooth stone slung from his sling shot. In another book, 2 Samuel 21:19–21 we read that "Elhanan son of Jair from Bethlehem killed Goliath of Gath," and that in another battle "there was a man of huge stature with six fingers on each hand and six toes on each foot...and Jonathan, son of David's brother, Shimeah, killed him when he defied Israel." Obviously, both David and two other warriors could not single-handedly be responsible for Goliath's death. This contradiction may be partially explained by remembering that the Bible is a series of traditions blended together. Some of the traditions overlap with others and repeat the same episodes. The scholars seem to think that David's reputation as the slayer of Goliath is a nice military fable. The Book of Chronicles, which is a magnificent whitewash of David's shadow side, does not even place him at the battle with the Philistines.

To interpret the text in a literal way is correct provided the reader has the literal meaning intended by the author. But to read the text with the surface literalness of a weather report can place the sincere reader in embarrassing positions. In this regard, how many believers of the Bible follow its injunction to become vegetarians? God said, "see I give you all the seed-bearing plants that are upon the earth, and all the trees with seed-bearing fruit; this shall be your food" (Genesis 1:29).

An easy example of literalness is Jesus warning about the rich man and the camel passing through the eye of a needle. "It is easier for a camel to pass through the eye of a needle than for a rich man to enter the kingdom of God" (Matthew 19:24). Passageways into the major cities of Israel were frequently given names. The Needle's Eye was the gate used by travelers and merchants. Thus we understand Jesus' image of the overburdened camel attempting to squeeze through the small toll gate of the city. A bit of geographical background and cultural information makes a world of difference from taking the text at face value.

The Bible, like every sacred scripture, is a second-hand exposition. The experiences recounted in the biblical writings are the fundamental revelation. Due to the various authors and the circumstances that called forth the writings, the Bible offers a range of meanings. It challenges readers because its authors wrote from various depths of meaning. From a careful reading one begins to gain insight into them. Dante, in his *Divine Comedy*, summarized the levels of meaning that Christian theologians and meditators had discovered over the centuries pondering the riches of the texts. He mentions:

> The scriptures can be understood, and ought to be explained principally in four senses. One is called literal...the second is called allegorical...the third sense is called moral...the fourth sense is called anagogical, that is, beyond sense; and this is when a scripture is spiritually expounded, which while true in its literal sense, refers beyond it to the higher things of the Eternal Glory...[1]

The Bible is written, as the Fathers of the Church and medievalists knew, for various levels of understanding. Taking only one perspective on the scripture and reading everything from only one point of view, surrounds the reader with inconsistencies and contradictions that are unexplainable on a word-for-word basis.

The complexity of the scriptures is there because the author is inspired, attempting to transpose a revelation, that is, an experience of divine origin, into human language. What greater disproportion could there be than to reduce a transcendental event to a few hundred human words? At this point the problem of expression contains two factors to reconcile: revelation and communication. How does one convey to an audience the meaning of an experience that radically exceeds customary routine?

Treating a sacred event with the tools of language, finding the images and phrases that convey its divine origin, preserving the right context of meaning for the benefit of the listener to make contact with the word of God, are all the pressured concerns of the writer. When God speaks in a single word, what author could explain it in less than 10,000 words? The experiencer wants to communicate the liberating event of revelation to others. How? To the former factors of expression must now be added symbolization and participation.

The only adequate way to describe the latent possibilities of scripture for various levels of authentic meaning is to recognize the flexible character of the sacred texts. Next to the revelatory experience itself—Moses before the burning bush, Jesus in the bright light at the top of Mount Tabor, the disciples awaiting the breath of the Spirit in the form of fire—the closest second-hand approximation is the effort to convey the event through symbolization.

The complex truths of scriptures reveal, in essence, a realm of reality, exceedingly intelligible, but disclosed by neither the senses nor discursive reason. The normal faculties for contacting the world at large are limited when it comes to the apprehension of divine truths. A sensible and rational rendering of the Bible can yield positive results. As Dante reminds us, however, there are significances unrevealed by rational investigation. Allegorical and moral significance are present in the texts. These levels of meaning require a certain finesse on the part of the reader, a certain sympathy or feeling for what the author intends. People who respect and strive for a virtuous life, for example, will discover the moral aphorisms pervading many passages. The Bible consoles. It serves as an uplifting source of inner nourishment for mind and heart. The texts, even at an elementary level, propose answers and questions asked by everyone. Matters of creation, the beginning of evil, human destiny, karmic consequences, the careers of sages and saints, are touched upon throughout the Bible. To pursue the truth further demands other skills.

From the biblical text itself, assertions and overtones point out that there is more to the words than the texts narrate. There are statements that leave the reader perplexed. What does saying, "the kingdom is within" have to do with my human nature? How does a modern person square scientific facts with scenes of power that exceed the normal course of action (the miracles)? Can a modern believer duplicate the feats attributed to the followers of Jesus?

The Bible states these unusual events without explaining them. The inability to answer the curious questions prompted by a fair reading of the texts has led to placing these supra-human demonstrations outside the reach of normal human attainment. This apparent disproportion between the event of revelation and the limitations of words may unfairly move the average reader to underestimate his or her own human potentials.

Revelation uses natural descriptions but the written word contains flashes of meaning that the unwary reader may easily miss. No amount of exegetical language study will suffice for unlocking these meanings. Many passages in scripture are truly not for the unprepared, the sincere believer who nevertheless does not possess the qualifications of discernment.

The tools for the literal meaning, for example, are different from the qualifications for the moral level. These levels are not interchangeable, although the second depends upon the first. Revelation in itself signifies an unveiling of divine origins. This experience takes outward shape for communication's sake in oral and written forms. Regardless of how ecstatic an experience may be, if I wish to communicate it to strangers I am forced to address them to a great extent on their home ground. Otherwise no communication takes place. The challenge is how to use finite words that convey infinite, divine reality. The arrangement of symbols is imperative.

Symbolic language implies more than words or their intellectual contents. A symbol is intelligible and meaningful to everyday life, without necessarily being rationally comprehended in all its aspects. One may speak of a courageous human, for example, as having a "lion's heart." Many nations have selected the eagle as their national symbol of power and government. In both instances, the symbolic meaning is more than just the reference to an animal and a bird as such. The significance of the symbol may require sufficient moral and intellectual preparation to ready one, as it were, to pierce its veiled truth.

The symbol's power resides in its ability to evoke hidden realities. In the very act of contacting the symbol, the mind grasps only partially the significance of the represented reality. The symbol's meaning and the mind of the interpreter is crucial, for the symbolic reality opens to a different kind of exegesis. This exegesis is the direct discernment of the writer's state of consciousness. It has little to do with professional degrees. Therefore the significance of the writer's vision is best appreciated by the reader whose mind is at the same level. Then the symbols reveal. The biblical sages illustrate this well.

The enrichment of the biblical insight, learning the message, requires other than academic qualifications. Sacred scripture is meant not to inform the reader about historical events but to touch the reader's life in a profound way. This kind of communication is not just the result of reading the words. At this juncture, the discipline of yoga can play an important role in biblical interpretation.

HOW YOGA PREPARES ONE FOR BIBLICAL INTERPRETATION

The practical import of yoga is the evolution of awareness. One becomes more adept at understanding the meaning of life, not as a result of information or additional concepts, but due to growth in awareness through the transformation of the conscious life force. There is a certain relationship here. The more one stimulates the life force, the more one becomes receptive. A ripening occurs that enables eyes to see and ears to hear. The actual power to grasp the meaning of life and be transformed by that meaning emerges through the practice of yoga. Since this growth affects the mind-body relationship, it cannot but help one in understanding sacred scripture.

As we have seen in a previous chapter, the five *yamas* and the five *nyamas* are foundational commitments that dispose the student for receptivity. These guidelines can produce a qualitative alteration in one's character that improves the art of biblical interpretation. A new integration of the vital dimensions arises as one progresses. Yoga especially concerns itself with improving the range and quality of human awareness. The power or capacity to apprehend meanings is, over time, greatly affected. In this way the reader's mind is prepared to be more sensitive to the richer meanings contained in biblical scenes. There is a kind of internal purification that stimulates the power of the mind to penetrate the mystery that life in itself reveals and that the Bible signifies. In this way, the depth of biblical interpretation flows from the depths of consciousness.

The lives of the prophets show an unusual degree of consciousness. Either they were strangely hallucinating or they gave remarkable evidence of power over nature and insight into the human condition. They spoke in a manner that conveyed to their audiences an inner vision that few recognized for themselves but many respected as genuinely important. Their performance emanated from a higher state of consciousness than their listening contemporaries. Their inner vision abided in their lives and continued to influence their judgments, often at the expense of seemingly more pragmatic solutions protested by their neighbors.

A NEW TYPE OF PARTICIPATORY EXEGESIS

While the Bible endorses a positive view of human beings' sublime nature, it seldom supplies the detailed steps to its full realization. The early commentators of the Bible, however, the laity and recluses of the Christian communities of the Egyptian and Palestinian regions, demonstrate in their writings an exegesis that directly contends with reaching the cosmic event.

The type of exegesis that allows for the final resolution of biblical symbol is direct participation in the reality symbolized. Scripture reveals in symbolic instances truths that are fully recognized only in the inner experience of spirit. The final level of exegesis is the individual's disciplined process of inspiration: one's spirit enters into itself consciously, thereby experiencing self-revelation. Inspired, literally filled with the spirit, all modes and degrees of the scriptural meanings become transparent. Inspiration becomes revelation—the same experience. The kingdom being within, one enters within consciousness to discover it. One crosses the border of time into the cosmic event. The inner experience transforms consciousness into an awareness of cosmic universality, wherein individual, relative truths, heretofore discovered and entertained by the rational faculty at its best, pale in comparison. Like the disciples, one becomes an "eyewitness." Perhaps this level of awareness is what Dante meant by "anagogical." The scriptures are sacred because the authors' conscious projections of their own illumined state reveal in symbolic fashion the divine significance of life. When one's consciousness is prepared to participate at this level of awareness, then the mystery of Christ-consciousness does not belong to the thrilling past; biblical truth is not faithfully admired only in memory. Like John on the island of Patmos, one has only to enter into one's own spirit to discover and reveal the cosmic mystery of the scriptures.

NAMING GOD

In any society there are social symbols that function as unifying elements. A country's flag, the mention of a hero's name, the recall of a catastrophic event can all exert an influence upon individuals or rally a community to action. Group memories and associations have a dramatic impact on people's lives. These experiences are preserved, utilized and summarized by most communities as a source of their identity. This ability to depict experiences of great value, to forge symbols, is found throughout cultures and histories.

Among Christians of every denomination, the use of religious language has been a source of identity and thus a bond of unity for believers. One of the most important symbols, if not the most crucial one, within any church community is the concept of God. The importance of this symbol among all Christians is its key position in their minds for justifying and unifying everything else about their beliefs and morals. The symbol "God" functions as the foundational belief and provides believers with their understanding of the meaning of life and death.

To appreciate the importance of symbols in society, however, as well as in religion, interpretation is required. The impact of symbols relies upon the tool of interpretation. Unless one interprets reality, life remains meaningless; with interpretation, life yields meaning. Without meaning one stands mute before the reality in question. Puzzlement transpires.

Through interpretation one deciphers the intelligibility of something—an action, a word, an idea—and arrives at a meaning about it. If my foreign friend has never seen a professional baseball game, it becomes my job to explain or decipher for him the symbols of the game—those actions and words used in the event, and without which the game can be neither understood nor enjoyed.

The marvelous quality of interpretation is that it can be conveyed to others. Meaning can be structured and transferred through symbols. Thus, communication takes place. In ordinary circumstances, the symbols of language work because they convey meanings. Normal conversation occurs not through sounds impinging upon the nervous system and brain but primarily through the exchange of meanings. The question "why" that the child repeats incessantly is another way of saying, "What does it mean?" Unless the sounds of words bear meaning, no interpretation is available. No communication results. Words are intelligible only because they are meaningful sounds.

Our lives are full of symbols. Human existence itself is the most symbolic of realities. Our conversation, our dress, our walk, our job, our leisure moments, our religion have meaning if only for ourselves. What we think, say and do possesses meaning because these activities are real. Since reality is the basis for meaning, what does not exist in some way has no meaning. My imagined thoughts, however, do have meaning since they are products of my real imagination, even though there may be no reference to reality outside my mind.

Meanings are expressed in symbols. To speak of a blue sky to a person blind from birth is meaningless. There is no experience of the reality with which to connect the two words.

I understand something because I can refer the explanation to my experience of the reality. People often emphasize the importance of their announcement by saying, "I speak from experience." The understanding or explanation is then cast into symbols. The symbol in turn derives its meaning from the "felt" experience. In this way people make life intelligible to themselves and articulate it to others. To understand something presupposes some experience of it.

The accepted ways people use symbols in society apply to those experiences in which they recognize or interpret the same meaning. Using symbols communicates meaning to the extent that the community shares sufficiently in a common experience. As a citizen, or member of a community, I know what you mean when you speak about something because I, like you, have some experience regarding the subject discussed. Ordinary human intercourse means that the participants sufficiently understand each other's use of symbols, having experienced the feeling of the symbols' meaning.

The Symbol God

The formative factors that have produced and are producing Western culture are not necessarily reinforcing the traditional beliefs in God. In fact, cultural life today mitigates the possibility of believing in God. This state of affairs does not imply a subtle and far-reaching atheistic plot against institutional Christianity; the phenomenon simply exists. There are discernible causes for this reduction of belief in God, but we will focus instead on examining the crisis for any positive signs of religious vitality. In a society that assumes newness and progress as basic to cultural survival, it should not come as a surprise that religious concepts change. Is it possible that a closer look at the symbol God as it occurs in our changing culture may reveal flaws?

The meaning of God as learned from religion classes and theology manuals may show a significance on paper, but there the relevance ends. In the factual condition of life today, this theoretic significance may be utterly unconnected to the daily struggles and ambitions of society. Theoretical coherence is not enough. The symbol God stands for ultimate and practical significance or it is not worth the time for consideration. To place this symbol into the market place, amidst the mass of factors shaping cultural life, demands a test for its applicability. Will belief in God stand up against life as it is experienced?

People are not so much doubting God's existence as they are God's meaning. For most people, higher values that transcend the corrosion of time are a necessity for a meaningful life. But in attempting to articulate these higher values, they are seriously looking at alternative options to the institutional concept or presentation of God. While every religion has its own portrait of God, the elaboration of the symbol must somehow relate to human experience.

Without this discernible reference to life as it is encountered, God remains a distant abstraction. If the symbol God stands for the completeness of life, the removal of privation and suffering, then asserting the symbol should do just that: complete life and remove suffering. It should achieve what it symbolizes.

Here, it seems to me, is the crux of the issue. Are religious symbols, especially that of God, realizable for people in their daily lives? Since God is the most comprehensible symbol in which one could believe, the activation of belief in that symbol should have comprehensive effects upon the life of the believer.

When human life is not being transformed by this most ultimate symbol known to civilization, there are basically only two reasons for that default. First, the believer is not engaging the symbol properly, somewhat like the child who reported to his parents that God is a "green bean." Upon checking the child's information, the parents discovered that the teacher referred to God as a "supreme being." While the implications of viewing God as a legume have never been documented, the failure of the symbol, in this instance, lies with the believer.

In addition to not being able to grasp the symbol of divinity correctly, there is a second, more crucial default. What if the symbol itself is incorrect? God in English is a three-lettered word; the Latin, *Deos*, is four-lettered; the Greek, *Theos*, is five-lettered; the Hebrew, *El*, is two-lettered. By themselves as combinations of four different alphabets, these words are relative to the culture. There is nothing sacrosanct in using just these letters. The letters forming the name God in the mind still mean different things to different people. Western religions, for example, have selected (interpreted) the contents of the word God. The God of the Calvinists is not the God of the Roman Catholics, nor is the God of the Lutherans the same as the God of Orthodox Jews. When yoga texts refer to *Ishwara*, sometimes translated as God, this designation means something very different from the denominational concept of the Christian notion of God. What makes the difference in all these instances is not the name but the meaning of the name.

The next question is, where did the meanings come from? The plural meanings of God prevailing today among believers may not be due only to the various denominational interpretations of God. Overlooked frequently is a prior consideration which affects the very construction of a symbol: the human mind.

While people speak and act symbolically, it is only their minds that catch the meanings contained in symbols. Without consciousness, there are no symbols expressed or apprehended. The construction of a symbol like God, however, puts a task upon the mind that is not required in everyday communication. The environment, for example, is sensibly and intelligibly available to the community. Public availability allows for a shared experience of life that is immediately referable for anyone's scrutiny. Words have a local character because the community uses them that way. When one lives in a region, one learns what they mean. The public availability to meaning can be experienced directly and immediately and can undergo alterations over time that the community recognizes. This public availability allows even strangers eventually to grasp the meaning of things. Local symbols become commonplace.

THE NAME FOR GOD

God is a different story. The criteria of public availability does not exist for apprehending the meaning of God. Neither Church, Synagogue, creed, liturgy nor Bible makes God knowable to the mind. In dealing with the God symbol, the mind is embarking on a necessary task that ironically exceeds it. The power of rationality tends to rely upon sensory images for conceiving its symbols. The images and concepts of the mind are drawn from our experience of daily living. We can invent new arrangements in our minds but these arrangements still use the same images and ideas drawn from life's experiences. It is exactly like designing a patchwork quilt. The patches of cloth can be arranged into many patterns, but each design uses the same patches.

A further dilemma looms. How can we compose a symbol when there seems to be no obvious grounding for it? Preaching the symbol does not explain it, but only enforces it through emotion. The problem of whether this symbolic version of God is meaningful remains unanswered. Today people are reluctant to assume the truth of religious statements because of authoritative force. It is not a resistance generated by anarchy, but a critical attitude that recognizes the inherent limitations of the mind. For Jews, Christians, and Mohammedans to insist that their symbol of God is the only acceptable one would be similar to producing a textbook on world geography that contained only maps of Jerusalem, Rome, and Mecca.

Any symbol of God is like a sandpail into which one tries to pour the ocean. The pail holds some water but it does not hold the ocean. When one holds onto an idea of God as the last word, one has made the pail equivalent to the ocean.

It may seem unfair, but every symbol of God involves a necessary illusion. The mind easily identifies its constructs with the reality that they represent. Wars have been fought over whose God is supreme. It is quite customary to assume that one's idea of God is the finest expression, the final word, on this sacred reality. In so doing, however, one succumbs to a deadly trap that the prophets of the Old Testament repeatedly warned their people against: the assumption that one concrete word is the exclusive symbol that designates God. That act of arrogance, for the prophets, qualifies as idolatry. An idea about the sacred becomes an idol, an illusion, when we misidentify it as being the reality. The map has become the territory.

Yet the believer's effort to portray God in concepts and images cannot be avoided. How else would there be communication? But if there is one universal agreement among all spiritual traditions (not necessarily institutional Churches), it is the declaration that the ultimate origin of the universe is beyond a detailed description. If God does not exceed the range of human images and concepts, then humans make God into their own image and thus worship an idol of their own construction.

There is an unresolvable tension in attempting to name divinity. The divine origin of life and the universe, on the one hand, is incomprehensible, while the human mind, on the other hand, deals with finite realities. The riddle of existence exceeds one's rational mind because it possesses too much intelligibility for one to grasp. That's why it is a mystery. The discursive mind grasps things in bits and pieces. Human learning takes place in steps. Although modern societies are run on electricity, no scientist is bold enough to assert that he has the complete story on electro-magnetism. If the world at large presents enigmatic challenges to our knowing it, how much more does its divine author?

Since human experience on a day-to-day basis constantly deals with finite, changing things, how does one even imagine an infinite, eternal reality? It is true that philosophers and theologians speak of divine attributes like infinity, omniscience, omnipresence, eternal in their description of God. But what do these terms mean in their minds when their world of experiences is just the opposite of these attributes? Equally, what do the biblical writers mean when they offer a panoply of symbols to describe God?

> I am that I am (Exodus 3:14)
> Fair (Psalms 27:4)
> God of gods and Lord of lords (Psalms 136:2,3)
> Eternal (Deuteronomy 33:27)
> Giver of life (Genesis 1:20)
> Holy of holies (Isiah 6:3)
> Wisdom (Proverbs 8)
> Wrathful (Psalms 88:16)
> Surpassing all things in greatness (Isiah 40:1)

They also declare God in poetic, anthropomorphic and nature terms:

> A star (Revelations 22:16)
> Fire (Deuteronomy 4:24)
> Sun (Psalms 84:11)
> Water (Psalms 84:6)
> Wind (John 4:24)
> Cloud (Exodus 13:21)
> Dew (Hosea 14:5)
> A still breeze (1 Kings 19:12)
> A stone (Psalms 118:22)
> Father (John 20:17
> Mystery (Daniel 2ff)
> A Lion (Hosea 11:10)
> Mother (Isiah 66:13)

These different names apply depending upon what portion of the Bible one reads. Yet no tradition within the Bible would claim that its presentation of God is utterly adequate. There seems to be no symbol in scriptures that adequately portrays the totality of God's meaning. God remains the *mysterium tremendum*, the "awesome mystery" that defies conceptualization. If one goes outside the

Christian scriptures and examines even older scriptures, the same descriptions are found. In the *Vedas*, ten-thousand-year-old scriptures, one reads:

> Exceedingly wise, exceedingly strong is the Designer.
> He is creator, disposer, epiphany supreme.
> He is our Father who begot us, he the Disposer
> who knows all situations, every creature. (Rig Veda 10:82)

> The Inspirer of all men advances, the Sun,
> displaying his mighty shimmering banner. (Rig Veda 7:63)

> He who is called Divine Friend brings men together.
> The Divine Friend supports both earth and heaven,
> watching over people, never closing an eye. (Rig Veda 3:59, 1)

> Behold the marvelous mystery of God.
> Near though he is, one cannot leave him.
> Near though he is, one cannot see him.
> He does not die, nor does he grow old. (Atharve Veda 10:8/332)

In the *Bhagavad Gita*, we read:

> I am the sacrifice and the offering, the sacred gift and the sacred plant. I am the holy words, the holy food, the holy fire, and the offering that is made in the fire. (Bhagavad Gita 9:16)

> Consider my sacred mystery: I am the source of all being, I support them all, but I rest not in them. Even as the mighty winds rest in the vastness of the ethereal space, all beings have their rest in me. Through my nature I bring forth all creation, and this rolls around in the circles of time, but I am not bound by this vast work of creation. I am and I watch the drama of works. (Bhagavad Gita 9:5–9)

Quite literally, there are few descriptions in the Bible that cannot be found in other world scriptures referring to the divine reality. The Hebrews and Christians were neither the exclusive nor the first composers of their revered symbols. Compiling all the symbols in both traditions that refer to God would still not add up to disclosing the full meaning of the eternal reality. Due to the limitations of any symbol, there can hardly be an ideal symbol for God. The meaning of symbol as symbol indicates that the mind recognizes there is always more to the referent than the reference tells. One suspects a surplus meaning that still needs further elaboration. If we overlook the surplus, then we easily assume that our symbol is the complete one.

Unless the believer who searches for divine symbols recalls that there is more than his or her conceptualization, then s/he partakes of an illusion. If one is sure of the total meaning of God, then one represses all other possibilities. No analogies, similarities, or substitutes are acceptable. There looms, then, the implicit danger that the believer believes too much. The God symbol becomes a ruse for its possessor. We often invent symbols that possess a meaning that is total, precisely because we invented the meaning. For instance, the design of a computer program possesses only that meaning which the programmer puts into it. The divine reality, however, is *totaliter aliter*—wholly other than any symbol that could ever be invented.

Attempting divine symbols would then seem an impossible task. Are there any guides, remote or otherwise, to render clues to knowing divine reality? In religious language and theological statements, one might use an ancient principle, namely, that one should never expect more clarity and certainty than the subject matter allows. At the same time, there is a coefficient factor that accompanies the principle: one cannot make music more beautiful than the instrument permits. Human subjectivity enters into all our efforts to be objective. What appeals to us about the God symbol learned at Sunday school may later become peripheral as we mature into life. The composition of our religious symbols should reflect our struggles with uncovering meaning in life. The stories in the Bible are packed with this diversified approach to God. As we grow up we assume uncritically many ideas and feelings about our environment, people, and destiny. Our cherished notions about divine realities are not insulated against this growth process. We subtract and we add to the meaning of life. Even with an intelligent and conscientious respect for life, certain meanings about reality do not show up until the time is ripe. Ripening is usually a lengthy and uneven process of struggling with life's experiences. What someone grasps in the symbol of God as a single adult is not always a duplication of one's religious thoughts in childhood, and even further from one's thoughts of God after becoming a parent. Rival notions of God could hardly not be expected in society.

How strange to find in the Old Testament a monstrously repulsive and brutal characterization of God that inspired Moses' followers to pillage and rape the promised land in his name:

> Why have you spared the life of all the women?...Kill all the male children, kill also all the women who have slept with a man. Spare the lives only of the young girls who have not slept with a man and take them for yourselves...This is a statute of the law which Yahweh has commanded Moses (Numbers 31:15ff).

Later we listen to the prophet Isaiah describe a God of irrevocable love and tenderness for his creatures:

> Now your creator will be your husband...Yes, like a forsaken wife distressed in spirit, Yahweh calls you back. Does a man cast off the wife of his youth? says your God. I did forsake you for a brief moment, but with great love will I take you back (Isaiah 54:5-6).

If the Hebrews had settled for their initial attempts to fathom the meaning of God, then scripture would not have gotten beyond portraying God as an obscene, tribal warrior.

The multitude of symbols found in the scripture suggests the varied attempts of human endeavor to overcome the limitations of the mind in discovering and expressing the meaning of God. The narratives that name God in scripture never tell the reader why that particular symbol is used. The symbols that relate to the natural surroundings and events of the time are an interpretation. Those of us who examine the Bible today are therefore obligated to fathom a limited interpretation. One's familiarity with nature and history is presupposed in order to appreciate the corresponding symbols describing God. We seem to know instinctively that our survival as well as our personal growth through life's experiences make it a necessity for reinterpreting again and again, ceaselessly, the meaning of existence.

God symbols cannot be otherwise than indefinite and unfinished, subject to revision, since they reflect the stages of our self-understanding. The need for reinterpretation is a safety measure against the smug complacency of those who have God, like life, all figured out. Even the disruptions of life can awaken the interpretive opportunity for knowing the ultimate mystery a little better.

Descriptions of God from varied spiritual traditions are to our benefit. They preserve the mind's suppleness. We recognize that although genuine symbols insinuate the divine reality, they cannot summarize the wholly other. By examining the multi-directions of these symbols, we stand a better chance of correcting our superstitions and clarifying the meaning of life's destiny. "But there are some great souls who know me. Their refuge is my own divine nature. They love me with a oneness of love; they know that I am the source of all" (Bhagavad Gita 9:13). When one has this kind of consciousness, then the communicative symbols one chooses will be an accurate, but partial, glimpse to inspire others.

THE MASTER DISCIPLE TRADITION

Since the Christian tradition encompasses a 2000-year-old history, it should not be surprising that there are many things in the tradition that are not remembered today. Among the forgotten truths of Christianity is the fundamental relationship that Jesus developed with his close followers: the Eastern relationship of master and disciple. Because it is unknown in Western culture, a modern reader reads about it but misses this relationship in the biblical scenes. In the West we note the biblical narratives that use terms like master, Lord, disciple, apostle, follower, without always realizing their significance in their day. Nowhere, in this author's survey, among theological writings nor in the religious mentality of typical Christians does one find an appreciation for the apprenticeship of master and disciple.

By inspecting the cultural meaning of the Gospel words in their textual use, one can hopefully gain an important understanding for our times.

CHRISTIAN FAITH: THE PREROGATIVE OF GOD

Christian denominations seriously foster a tradition of communicating religious content to their converts. And yet every denomination exhibits an ambivalence toward communication. On the one hand, churches express their religious concern for proper indoctrination. On the other, those chiefly responsible for instruction—the bishops, ministers, priests, nuns, teachers, parents—are the first to admit that the principal and exclusive agent for communicating faith is God. Only God gives the gift of conversion. Only God draws the woman or man to himself through faith in Jesus. People hear the biblical word and are moved by the divine gift of faith. It is the Christian God who somehow, mysteriously, disposes the recipient for belief. God remains sovereignly free, transcendent to human pressure or solicitation. Understandably, then, Christians view themselves as the receivers of God's good will, totally dependent upon that will prevailing. One is understandably impressed that the disposal of faith remains entirely God's initiative.

A critique of this kind of religious communication is that it makes no real allowance for human participation. If God does what he will, then why should those authorities responsible for religious indoctrination be so conscientious? In the context that God's grace is all, the role of the religious educator would hardly be more than an external supporter.

This emphasis upon God's sole agency questions the necessity of a human teacher as well as the active participation of the convert, beyond that of merely seconding the motion. The serious reduction of the human agency makes of faith an instantaneous, magical force in the recipient with the human teacher and the aspirant playing merely receptive roles. Only God, in other words, produces the miracle of making that alteration in human consciousness called faith. When this model of religious communication between God and a potential believer is transposed to the Gospels, Christian indoctrination would have its members believe that Jesus is the active teacher and the disciples the passive believers. It is this typical faith model of God as active agent and the believer as passive recipient that needs examination.

THE MEANING OF DISCIPLE: APPRENTICESHIP

In the New Testament there are many scenes that involve Jesus' role as teacher to his followers. The believers that Jesus chose to instruct are given a specific designation: the Greek word, *mathetes*, or "disciple," which is used 197 times. We are familiar with the words "disciple" and "master" as these words appear in the English translations of the Greek Bible. Yet we have little use for the word "master" in English today. Master of the house or master-teacher are anachronisms in Western culture. In the East, however, the term persists. There, one can legitimately refer to qualified individuals as master artists, masters in martial arts, or spiritual masters. This notion of master is quite common in the Middle East as well. Jewish rabbis, for example, have always been known as masters.

The concrete meaning of master (Greek, *didaskelos*) conveys more than competence in a field of art or learning. When used with the word *didaskein*, "to apprentice," it appears 49 times in the Gospels and implies a special relationship with students. Throughout the biblical texts when Jesus is referred to as master with his student disciples, the word *didaskein* is always employed. Unfortunately the rich meaning of the Greek does not come through in the English text. The English often translates the Greek by the word "teaches," which does not convey the meaning of apprenticeship. It is true that the function of *didaskein* is teaching, but our twentieth-century use of the word does not capture the impact of its use in its original context.

When a master chooses to accept someone as a student, that person commits himself and his lifestyle to the requirements of the master. This profound relationship between master and disciple has nothing to do with registering for courses and attending formal classes. As much as possible, the relationship becomes a daily, lived association. The disciple is a disciple only because he apprentices to the master. The British use of apprenticeship approaches, but does not convey the wide intensity of the Eastern notion.

Biblically, to be called a disciple, *matketes*, means that one apprentices, *didaskein*, to a master, *didaskelos*. This relationship implies much more than our fondest memories of a teacher-student episode in high school or college. Apprenticeship is more akin to the rapport between parent and child, where the child strives to model himself upon the parent in a day-to-day association.

Discipleship further implies that one undergoes systematic practices with the guidance of the master who is accomplished in them. Apprenticing a student does not mean conveying information. It includes, but is profoundly more than, an intellectual endeavor. The disciple is one who is trained and transformed. There is a continuous regimen implied in the meaning of apprenticeship.

Interestingly, the New Testament uses the word apprentice 97 times without once designating the skill involved. When the word is used without a referent, then the tacit implication allows for a specific interpretation in the Jewish culture. The apprenticeship focuses upon the acquisition of the holiness and wisdom of the Torah. Quite emphatically, Jesus asserts his role in regard to the Torah: "Do not imagine that I have come to abolish the Torah or the Prophets. I have come not to abolish but to complete..." (Matthew 5:17). Into that completion he draws his disciples.

Torah is often translated as Law. The English-speaking reader obviously invests the word "law" with juridical overtones. The Torah, however, has no connection with a formal piety governed by law. Torah means knowing the divine ways so that one becomes transformed by them. To know the Torah is an existential knowledge that touches the whole person. Learning the Torah had little to do with memorizing the words of Moses and the prophets. Keeping that orientation in mind, Matthew's entire Gospel emphasizes that Jesus identified his mission with the implementation of the Torah. As a master of the Torah, his business was to demonstrate how one could attain the purpose of the Torah, namely, to become as perfect as one's heavenly Father (Matthew 5:48). More than intellectual familiarity or compliance with liturgical rites, the learning of the Torah required a personal transformation, to be filled with the spirit of holiness.

In his role as master of the Torah, Jesus is referred to in the Gospels as "master," *didaskelos*, 45 times. Insufficient attention has been noted in the Gospel texts that record "master," not as one of many titles, but as the most frequent title given to him. These texts indicate that he was involved in the preparation of a group of people who would assist him with his mission. This preparation is best understood by readers today in recalling the Eastern mentality in its understanding of the master-disciple apprenticeship. This model, as we will see, brings out meanings that conventional Christian theology overlooks in Jesus' relationship with his selected group.

To aid the reader further in showing the importance of the word "master," let us contrast it with the designation of Jesus as prophet. The word "prophet," *prophetes*, is applied to Jesus only 13 times in the Gospels. From a study of the Gospel stories, Jesus does engage in prophetic utterances. Yet the citing of him as master occurs with such frequency that the New Testament writers leave no doubt about which functional role assumed emphasis. In the Jewish culture the prophet publicly announced religious news that affected the community's spiritual survival. He spoke to the crowds, seeking to deliver a message, a wake-up call, in an oratorical style that moved the people to action. His urgent appeal was not in the interest of attracting followers, but rather in the interest of jarring minds to change the direction of their lives.

The master's approach was entirely different. He gradually gathered a select group. His instructions were not so much in delivering a timely message as in instilling ways for his trainees to alter their perspective of reality, and from this self-knowledge pursue their life work. The prophet's concern for his audience is to arouse them, to take the message to heart. In shaking people up, the prophet was not always appreciated. He is not interested in acquiring disciples. The master concerns himself with the state of mind and lifestyle of his disciples, but with an intensity and intimacy that is reserved exclusively for them. Jesus enacted both roles, speaking often to the public as a prophet, and to his disciples as a master.

THE SIGNIFICANCE OF SITTING

The Gospels narrate:

> Seeing the crowds, he went up the mountain. There he sat down and was joined by his disciples. Opening his mouth, he apprenticed them...(Matthew 5:1–2).

> Daily in the temple courtyard, I sat apprenticing...(Matthew 26:55).

The posture of sitting is a traditional one found in the East. One could officiate at a synagogue or lecture to crowds from a standing position. Sitting, however, was a sign of a special activity. To sit meant that the master was ready to apprentice his students. Yogis trained in the traditional master-disciple association soon discover that a genuine teacher should be able to sit quietly for a very long time. Moreover, a teacher will not teach someone who fidgets and constantly alters his or her posture. The quieting of the body means that there is an internal calmness of mind disposed now to listen and absorb the teachings.

In the most ancient spiritual tradition of the Himalayas, sitting near a master in this manner is called, in Sanskrit, *upanishad*. The recorded oral transmission, *smrti*, of the ancient sittings were collected under the title *Upanishads*. These writings were the *vedanta*, the cream of the *Vedas*. They summarized the realized wisdom of the *vedic* seers. The masters would initiate their chosen students or *chelas* into the ways in which the trainee would personally arrive at the same universal insight. Teaching the *Upanishad* meant an apprenticeship for the disciple who embarked upon a strict training program that involved body, mind, and spirit. The goal of this master-disciple apprenticeship was to bring the *chela's* level of consciousness to the self-same awareness that pervaded the Upanishadic master.

In the collection of *Upanishad* scriptures, a reader can peruse the stories and statements which distill the original state of consciousness. The actual training methods, those psychosomatic exercises that eventually produce the conversion to a new state of consciousness, are excluded. These revered practices—*sadhana* or *prayoga shastras*—are the essence of the apprenticeship. These practices are deftly inculcated to the disciple when the master views the disciple as ready. It is the disciple's job to establish him/herself in them. In that way, the disciple experiences the power of their meaning. Involved throughout the training is a complex relationship that affects the entire lifestyle of the student.

The student's faith, *shraddha*, in the master is never passive. At first, the student may have reservations and doubts. But as s/he prepares himself by the daily assimilation of the prescribed practices, s/he experiences the results within. S/he will note how emotions, thinking, judgements, and energy levels are undergoing vast changes. From these indisputable biological, psychological, mental, and spiritual permutations, confidence in them and the master grows. Faith concludes evermore in lived experience. With the disciple's progressive assimilation of the psychodynamic practices, the master can lead the student even further. Unless the disciple practices, there is obviously no assimilation; the master's power cannot be a surrogate for the incompetence of the disciple. Advanced practices would be withheld since the integrated readiness is absent. Whence the Gospel admonishment: "Many are called but few are chosen" (Matthew 22:14). Superior athletes and artists recognize eventually the indispensable necessity of undergoing an *ascesis*, an unrelenting, self-training that alters the biological and psychological make-up of the individual so that the person can withstand the energy demands required for exceptional performance.

Spiritual training is even more demanding. The chosen ones qualify by their determined efforts. They have made themselves ready. The questionable believer is on the verge of becoming the experienced disciple.

The *upanishadic* experience of sitting near the seer has been the model for the yoga master throughout the centuries. It is the accepted norm when a teacher desires to impart universal wisdom. At times the conduct and words of the master seem rationally indefensible. The student goes through periods of doubt and suspicion, even resentment. The master constantly challenges the rigidity of outlook as when Jesus cautions James and John about being destructively competitive because someone outside the group was getting equal results. Throughout all the vicissitudes of the apprenticeship, the master will advise the student: if the disciple is not benefiting, or if the master is selfish, then the student should quickly depart.

CONTEMPORARY MISREADING OF THE GOSPELS

Our analysis of the master-disciple relationship shows that a direct English reading into the texts does not convey the proper meaning of these terms. The usual interpretation by Christians of the master-disciple passages carries the impression that Jesus was an instructor giving lessons in religious information. Among church denominations emphasizing biblical indoctrinations, Jesus is seen to have preached to believers. Then, to ensure that the disciples got the message, God worked mysteriously in their minds the disposition necessary to accept Jesus' instructions. The disciples then received the faith which transformed their lives. This encounter resembles a passive process in which the disciple's personal initiative counted little.

To the contrary, an entirely different perspective is constant in the textual elaboration of the master-disciple relationship. Jesus initiates his chosen students into a discipleship which revolutionizes their consciousness. They train themselves under his guidance in performance skills that were to match his own:

> He who believes in me will also do the works that I do and greater works than these will he do (John 14:12).

Modern Christians do not view themselves as trainees but as believers. They are followers of Jesus like the crowds mentioned in the scriptures. Jesus spoke to these people but he did not consider them his disciples. The crowds may have believed and hoped in the words of Jesus but they could not realize the achievement of the disciples without the necessary apprenticeship. The question that emerges today is: What has happened to the tradition of apprenticeship in the churches? Where does one find the performance skills demonstrated by the disciples in the book of Acts?

FAITH AND APPRENTICESHIP

If there is a single word that characterizes the disposition that Jesus' followers had towards him during his public life, it was "faith." The English language uses two words—faith and belief—for the original Greek meaning of the verb, *pisteuein*, which means "to believe." Thus one speaks of having faith or the act of believing. Scholars admit that the New Testament writers preserve the Greek meaning exactly. The various meanings that faith possesses in the minds of contemporary Christians is more a denominational preference than an analysis of the biblical sense of the word.

Placing faith within the context of apprenticeship underscores a meaning of faith that is not obvious in the churches today. Faith in its Greek usage conveyed the meaning "to trust," "to rely on." In this sense of the word, a disciple's entrance into the apprentice relationship would require faith. After all, he is a beginner, a recruit, a raw neophyte. In listening to a speaker or coming into the presence of a dynamic teacher, one can feel the attraction toward the person. The speaker's presence and message can draw an angry or an admiring crowd. Individuals may want to pursue further their spontaneous acceptance of this personage. All the reasons for the attraction may not be rationally evident until later reflection. Somehow, though, the listener was touched by the experience. This positive disposition to trust in the speaker is "faith" for the Greeks.

Belief, then, is quite an ordinary response in daily life; one accepts another person for himself and for what he stands. The more exposure to a person, the more one's trust or mistrust grows. In this way credibility becomes established or abolished. It can apply similarly to trusting or having faith in oneself. In English, we apply the word "confidence" to ourselves, meaning "with," *con* "trust," *fides*. Having personal confidence means we trust ourselves.

The initial phase of an apprenticeship could very well be either infatuation or a certain ambivalence. One could be emotionally thrilled by the teacher's message and thus believe uncritically, or one could be intrigued and yet have reservations. Either response would be understandable. Unfortunately, today many religious instructors present the Good News to people in the form of a dilemma: either believe or go to perdition.

When Jesus announced his vision of life, there is recorded in the scriptures a whole spectrum of responses. Some felt hostility, others were awed. A few decided to entrust themselves for awhile and become apprenticed to him: "Immediately they left their nets and followed him" (Matthew 4:20).

The act of faith is the ordinary human initiative to trust another person. Faith is one's choice. As the relationship develops, there will, no doubt, be opportunity for correcting earlier presuppositions. In the Eastern tradition of *guru-chela*, master-student relationship, the master is very much aware of the student's struggle with faith. The master carefully guides the student through life experiences that challenge his or her current understandings. These life experiences become the vehicle for learning about how the student imposes self restrictions, expanding them to self-awareness. Clarification is not always sweet and easy. Nevertheless, the disciple must struggle with the understanding of reality in order to fathom the master's teachings. Without inner struggle, faith remains vague and delusional.

Faith in the master, however, amounts to more than an abstract credal statement. The circumstances of the master-disciple interplay involve a series of trying experiences for the aspirant. The cunning master assesses with clarity the specific ingredients necessary for the student's spiritual improvement. The disciple fails, at times, to comprehend the master's deeds and words. Insight comes hard. Obstacles are self-imposed. The master often appears unorthodox. The master's ways sometimes baffle, since the disciple is so limited in the conception of spiritual growth. The master's purpose is not to check the disciple's enthusiasm but to encourage him or her to follow out the implications of the practices. The disciple's improved understanding of the lessons of life follows less upon the master's inspiring words then upon his personal practices.

These spiritual practices, sadhana, produce in the practitioner the dynamic inner alteration that enables a new vision of life. In their use, the exercises heighten the practitioner's capacity for self-knowledge, bringing about drastic changes. Practice affects vision. The disciples of Jesus, for example, were taught how to use their inner energy for the plight of the ill and crippled. Through the experience of this dynamic ability, the disciples would not only realize anew their own worth, but appreciate the value of their master. It is in this marvelous display of their independent powers that the disciples are enabled to estimate how far they have come in their apprenticeship and learn its worth.

On occasions when the master, Jesus, would demonstrate his wondrous healing powers to the disciples, they would naturally be more in awe than comprehension. Later, after being trained in the augmenting and use of this inner power, they could realize that they, too, shared in the same life force. Contemporary theology unfairly places the miraculous events narrated in the gospels beyond the pale of ordinary believers. In a sense this is true. Most believers, then as now, would not have undergone the necessary training to prepare themselves for expressing this inner force. Being unfamiliar with the possibility and nature of this human power, believers view it as exceeding their competence. In other words, they have no faith in themselves. This kind of deficiency reflects in the puzzled reactions narrated in the gospels about Jesus' identity. The problem is not with the master's proficient and discreet exposure of his power. The problem is with the believers' lack of faith in themselves. As long as the disciples have self-doubts, these weaknesses confound their understanding of the master's identity. Without self-trust, without relying upon the human power within themselves, the disciples remain constrained by their suspicions and weak in their resolve. Thus, the master remains an enigma: Who do men say I am? (Matthew 16:13).

Faith by itself does not transform. Faith fosters the mental attitude and emotional readiness not to limit the possibilities of human consciousness. The disciple says, in effect, "I will trust, train, and see what happens." Faith is like assuming a hypothesis. Although all the proof is not available yet, one goes about life as though the thesis were self-evident. In time the feedback from the training will prove the thesis either way. It is the master's business to challenge any cultural and personal restrictions within the disciple's mind that restrains his or her potential growth. Through words and deeds and especially through silence, the master coaxes, pressures, stimulates, even commands the disciple to continue practicing until the hypothesis is proven through experience. Faith collapses into self-evident conviction.

THE DISCIPLES' FAILURE

A disciple's association with the master will have human feelings about it that need correction and maturing. Students often fantasize about their spiritual progress and the power of their master. Infatuation leads to exaggeration. Having made the same mistakes, the master knows how difficult it is to stay grounded in reality. Consequently, s/he will not be averse to selecting harsh measures to bring students back to the facts of life. Apprenticeship is not easy; it is strenuous and prolonged. There are moments of disillusionment; the master does not necessarily fulfill the student's expectations.

Revering the master is not enough. Having faith in the master is an elementary beginning. Fervent admiration may provoke interest but it will not effect transformation. The master does not need praise. The master desires the disciples' actualization of their inherent capacities. The master assists the process; s/he is not a substitute for it. The work of apprenticeship is, above all else, the disciple's efforts leading to new self-discovery.

An illustration of this principle of self-training occurs dramatically in the gospels. Having performed successfully in the art of healing, the disciples take on a new challenge and utterly fail. They are obviously chagrined at this embarrassing situation. Matthew's account of their failed attempt to cast out a demonic influence from a boy (Matthew 17:14–20) becomes for Jesus the master the occasion for teaching a profound lesson.

The boy's father, still seeking a cure, implores Jesus to rectify the lad's disturbance. He relates also how the healers-disciples failed to do the job. In response, Jesus stuns everyone involved: "Faithless and perverse generation! How much longer must I put up with you?" (Matthew 17:17). In spite of this rebuke, he cures the boy. No explanation is given for his exclamation. Instead, the gospel narrator depicts a later scene where the disciples are apparently alone with Jesus and they press him: "Why were we unable to expel it?" (Matthew 17:20).

Let us interject here. If these disciples understood healing the way modern Christians do, then they should have revised the question along these lines: "Why did not God work through us to heal the boy?" or "Why did not you, our master, extend your divine power through us as your instruments and thus effect a cure?" There is no hint at this interpretation. On the contrary, the disciples expected to cure the boy. They were experienced in healing; it was not their first attempt. Did Jesus hold back some technique required in this instance? Did the disciples, as it were, run out of healing power? Did God ordain to hold his grace of healing from the disciples' efforts? Speculation could wander in many directions.

Jesus' reply to their consternation is almost too simple. The disciples failed because they had too "little faith." Then Jesus makes his point with his faulty students: "If your faith were the size of a mustard seed, you could say to this mountain, 'move from here to here,' and it would move; for nothing would be impossible to you" (Matthew 17:21)

The striking use of the metaphor, mountain, would remind the disciples of their prodigious potential. Physically moving a mountain seems absurd. Yet if the disciples could overcome their lack of faith, less than seed size, even a mountain could not resist them.

The question of weak faith pertains to themselves. Jesus does not remind his disciples that they should pray next time and then God will work his healing miracle through their humble submission. In fact, earlier he advised them not to multiply prayers (Matthew 6:7) and not to pray in public

(Matthew 6:5). Jesus does not hint at their lack of faith in himself or in God; the issue is much closer to them—their lack of faith in themselves. Their question was not why did God fail to act in and through us, but why did "we" fail. Jesus is not trying to instruct them in the idea that they are nothing and God does it all. The disciples' failure to procure the anticipated healing is not God's fault; it's nothing less than a failure of nerve. Jesus bluntly tells them they do not have enough trust in themselves. He reminds them that they, not God, are to move mountains.

Jesus' sarcasm is consistent with the master-disciple model. The master's responsibility is not to pick up the pieces of his students' failures, but to induce in them the strength of self-confidence. If they do not build their self-trust, then their inherent powers remain sporadic and weak. His scolding reminds them just who is responsible.

Insisting in this way on the disciples' need for more self-determination does not detract from their acknowledgment of the Jewish God. Showing pious deference to God is not the issue. These students are being trained to discover and use their powers properly. Substituting God's agency in the face of a challenge to these powers dodges the purpose of their training.

Once the reader recognizes the consistent use of this master model in the gospels for designating Jesus' most frequent activity, then many other biblical passages become clarified. To the crowds, Jesus preached; to his disciples, he taught through the mode of apprenticeship. Unfortunately we are only given some of the highlights of their resultant practices and not the specific exercises that account for their achievements. Nowhere do the listed gospels narrate, for example, the specific techniques for healing. This reluctance of the gospel writers is also quite customary. Operational techniques are seldom revealed in writing. They are individually handed on to the prepared disciple, lest they be abused or trivialized in a public exposition. In the East, masters appraise their spiritual knowledge as a sacred trust.

The lingering question is, What has happened to that trust since the apostolic era? The master-disciple pattern of spiritual development has always been a personalized process whereby the disciple also matures into a master. Then s/he passes on, *traditio*, the spiritual heritage to his or her disciples. As Christianity developed after the first generation disciples, a double trend occurred. The new converts were initiated—baptized—into the mysteries of

Christianity and given their instructions and offices of responsibility. The Christian religion became slowly institutionalized with all the advantages and disadvantages that accompany consolidation.

In addition, the first two hundred years of Christianity showed an amazing diversity of emphasis and interpretation among the "followers of the way," as the Christians were then called. Already one finds a diverse, allowable emphasis mentioned in the Acts between Peter and Paul.

Among this spectrum of Christian followers was a thrust to continue a more meditative form of living. Groups of men and women formed communities, usually in the villages and rural areas rather than in the cities. Many individuals preferred to live more solitary lives and became mountain hermits. It was in this type of environment that the master-disciple association was preserved. Over the centuries this tradition likewise became structured and formalized into monasteries and convents in keeping with the vast organizational trend of Christianity. As Western culture and Christendom continued to interact over the years, the master-disciple pattern underwent changes. The clergy now assumed by their office as ordained ministers the rights and duties of spiritual guides, the self-training, the *ascesis*, was encouraged but the designation of the clerical office assumed the authority. Occasionally, the emergence of a saint in society would attract a cult following and people would be inspired to pattern their lives after this individual's example and words.

The monastic atmosphere and the growth of seminaries in modern times developed a type of preparation to meet the needs of the Church in its confrontation with modern, secular society. The ancient master-disciple pattern receded into amnesia. Officially, it was no longer endorsed. Modern times saw all the various denominations stress the need for devotional prayer and attendance at community services. Catholicism emphasized mandatory attendance at the sacraments as the principal means for spiritual growth since this approach was under the regulation of the clergy. Even in monasteries and convents, where there was still some echo of the older master-disciple association, it was still secondary to the formal sacramental activity of the monks and nuns, regulated by Canon law. The Protestant churches, in their various ways, shifted the emphasis to individual interpretation of the Bible and private acceptance of Jesus Christ as one's personal Savior.

There is still one area of Christianity, however, that reveres the older tradition of the master-disciple association. The Orthodox monasteries of Mount Athos preserve the tradition of the desert fathers. These monasteries on an extremely rugged mountain peninsula of Greece, have arranged their monastic lifestyles to draw upon the texts and techniques from the original hermits along with the writings of those saints they produced through the centuries. For those who have prepared themselves, cave life is also available.

While entrance into this ascetic lifestyle is restricted to celibate monks, there is today a definite but uneven return to the gospel pattern of master and disciple for a growing number of Christians. Due to the influence of writers like Thomas Merton, William Johnston, and Bede Griffith, Christians are becoming re-acquainted with the enlivening power of the meditative traditions. Nuns and ministers have joined the laity in entering into Eastern monasteries as disciples to learn yoga and zazen techniques of meditation from acknowledged masters. Some newer monastic foundations are deliberately structuring their mode of spiritual living along the lines of Eastern monasteries, *ashrams* and *zendos*.

These voluntary experiments in self-knowledge are answering an increasing desire in Christians to broaden their personal responsibility for their spiritual quest. If this healthy trend continues, then the twenty-first century may well see seekers transformed into saints and erudition expanded into enlightenment.

MIRACLES, SIDDHIS AND SCIENCE

During World War I some Arab tribes were exposed for the first time to the telegraph. They considered the event divinely miraculous, until someone taught them how to operate the device. Some years later, in an obscure village tucked away in the Italian Alps, a citizen returning from a trip to Rome informed the villagers that the United States had just placed the first man on the moon. Awestruck, the people quickly crossed themselves and declared a miracle. Everyone knew that man had no such power; only God ruled the heavens.

In their non-technological world view, both the Semitic tribe and the Italian villagers found it difficult to believe that humans could naturally fulfill these announcements. The presence of an electronic apparatus for the Arabs and the story of space travel for the Italians could not help but produce astonishment—which is the proper incentive for declaring miracles. Alas, when knowledge dawned, the miraculous vanished. For our villagers, knowledge and miracle offset one another.

Before explaining the yogic view of miracles, let us first review the contemporary understanding of miracles for Christians. The Christian tradition of the miraculous traces its origins to the miracles of Jesus and his disciples in the New Testament. Throughout the development of Christianity, however, various religious leaders have interpreted the tradition differently. Let us, for instance, reach back into the stirrings of Protestant Christianity for its explanation of miracles.

In his *Sermons on St. John,* Martin Luther mentions that:

> Apostles have preached the word and have given their writings, and nothing more than what they have written remains to be revealed, no new and special revelation or miracle is necessary.[1]

Luther's reading of scriptures led him to conclude that the days of the Christian miracle-working ceased with the death of the apostles. People of his time needed only to hear the word of the Lord, rather than witness wonders. Luther reminds us of the Pauline injunction that faith is acquired through hearing the word. Therefore converting men spiritually through the office of preaching was an immeasurably greater task than miracle working.

Another dominant influence in Protestantism, John Calvin, insisted that after the apostles, Christians were no longer permitted the power of miracles. He states in his *Institutes* that:

> The gift of healing disappeared with the other miraculous powers which the Lord was pleased to give for a time, that it might render the new preaching of the gospel for ever wonderful.[2]

A similar judgment upon miracles is echoed in contemporary theology by some of the most influential churchmen. Karl Barth's writings acknowledge the presence of miracles in the apostolic period but see no reason for God's power to enter into our world again on such a scale.[3] He insisted that God's holy spirit functions today only to dispose believers' minds to accept in faith the biblical episodes. This view is seconded by such notable theologians as Dietrich Bonhoeffer, Paul Tillich, and Bishop John A. T. Robinson.

But the contemporary school of thought that receives the largest following among scriptural scholars and churchmen today is Rudolph Bultmann:

> The whole conception of the world which is presupposed in the preaching of Jesus as in the New Testament generally is mythological, i.e., the conception of the world as being structured in three stories, heaven, earth, and hell; the conception of the intervention of supernatural powers in the course of events; and the conception of miracles, especially the conception of the intervention of supernatural powers in the inner life of the soul...[4]

According to Bultmann, modern people, living in a scientific age, must retain their critical sense in professing religion. The biblical world and its descriptions of events has little in common with our industrialized civilization. The modern believer must scale down the biblical "myths" in order that the gospel messages have an acceptance in our nuclear age. The biblical passages require what Bultmann calls "demythologizing": the miraculous dimension as a factual account must be rejected. The miracles did not happen. In reality, according to Bultmann, the faith of the early Christians was conveyed in mythological descriptions that appear to modern readers as concrete, miraculous events. Once we analyze the peculiarities of the biblical language and the unscientific, primitive world view possessed by the gospel writers, then we can understand the non-miraculous meaning behind these faith-created stories. Bultmann thought that one has to strip the mythological language away from the real event that took place in order to avoid the modern, superstitious evaluation that these events were miraculous.

Both Bultmann and Barth want to distinguish carefully two separate spheres of existence. God's existence in his absolute transcendence is opposite to humanity's in its frail, incomplete and transitory material world. The opposition is total and complete. The distance between human and God is an infinite abyss. Human nature is incapable of crossing it. By exaggerated confidence in their own ingenuity, humans only keep themselves from God. The only way to cross the abyss, for Barth, is by humanity's return to biblical faith. Humanity's world of arts and sciences cannot in any way enable people to reconcile themselves to God. Humanity's hope in itself ends in chaos, as seen in the event of World War I.

According to these theologians God is in heaven and humans are on earth—two different beings, two different kingdoms. Humanity's natural powers of intellect and will, which have fashioned their flawed technocratic world, are absurdly useless in making any kind of contact with the divine kingdom. The condition of humanity's inability to communicate with God is theologically and religiously known as its fallen and sinful condition. The only solution to this dilemma is through God's condescension to humanity in the form of Jesus Christ, sent by the Father to redeem the situation. Humanity is saved from the confines of its corrupt nature and limited worldview through faith in Jesus, who by his perfect nature as the God-man breached the abyss. Christian faith in Jesus saves humans from their tragic isolation on earth and provides an emancipatory meaning to human existence.

Barth views miracles as belonging to God's exclusive power. He affirms that these wondrous events manifested in the human world during the apostolic period, but for him the attestation of miracles ceases there. Bultmann equally emphasizes the role of faith in human deliverance from its fallen condition. But he prefers a different evaluation for the apostolic period, which apparently recorded miraculous events. Some excerpts from his main essay, "Kerygma and Myth," establish his intellectual judgement on the problem of miracles:

> Man's knowledge and mastery of the world have advanced to such an extent through science and technology that it is no longer possible for anyone seriously to hold the New Testament view of the world....The miracles of the New Testament have ceased to be miraculous....It is impossible to use electric light and the wireless and to avail ourselves of modern medical and surgical discoveries, and at the same time to believe in the New Testament world of spirits and miracles.[5]

For Bultmann, the danger of insisting upon these biblical "myths" lies in presenting an unintelligible and unacceptable Christian faith to modern sophistication.

He sees our present day scientific understanding as an essential criteria with which to judge the early apostolic writers. He does not think that these writers falsified their narratives, but rather that the imagery and figures of speech in the ancient Semitic-Roman world were the only descriptions available to be utilized by the faith interpretation of these Christian authors. Since modern understanding of energy and matter could not be available in their culture, how could they be held literally responsible for appealing to the modern mind? If modern science truly understands today's world, then a Christian cannot be a fundamentalist about the Bible. Even more than Barth, Bultmann insists that no divine agency would interrupt the natural laws of our cosmos. The ignorance of the workings of nature in past cultures is continuously rectified by the advances of scientific progress.

From our overview of Western Christianity three basic theories regarding miracles can be seen:

1. *Apostolic Dispensation.* In this theory God allowed miracles in order to establish the credibility of the Christian church during the apostolic period. These miracles reinforced Jesus' message. Once the church was secure in the Mediterranean area, God withdrew his dispensation.

2. *Mythological.* In this theory the miracles did not happen in a concrete, literal manner. The miracle passages of the Bible are not factual accounts but symbolic descriptions. When Jesus cured the blind man, for example, this incident should be read as spiritual blindness; the raising of the dead points out that one who is dead in spirit may recover religious life anew. This theory depicts the miracle stories as allegorical descriptions. Theories 1 and 2 are held by most mainline Protestant churches.

3. *Divine Intervention.* In this theory the biblical passages are accurate accounts. Yet throughout history as witnessed by saintly people and special places (Lourdes, Fatima, other shrines, holy articles and relics of saints), God has intervened and permitted a dispensation of his power beyond the apostolic period for special people and occasions. This view is generally held by Roman Catholic churches.

While most modern theologians of mainline denominations would concur with the above threefold division, there are, nonetheless, Christian groups who have considered miracles as a normal functioning of their evangelizing. The Pentecostal, Fundamentalist, and Christian Science churches, for example, have always recognized and even encouraged the divine phenomenon of "healing" miracles. Currently, there is also the trend known among many different denominations as the Charismatic movement. Among these believers, the power of the Christian God, in some mysterious manner, may affect relief or a cure for an ill person. Usually, these positive results require the instrumental aid of the official minister or designated healer within the group. But any authentic miracles of healing are attributed solely to divine agency: the divine intervention persists in history and, on the basis of its scriptural interpretation, may be called down upon the Christian community.

MIRACLES IN THE NEW TESTAMENT

A miracle in the traditional sense certainly isn't an ordinary occurrence in our times. For Saint Augustine a miracle meant:

> something difficult, which seldom occurs, surpassing the faculty of nature and going far beyond our hopes as to compel our astonishment.[6]

Derived from Latin, the word miracle means "something admirable," or "extraordinarily wonderful," an event that would not be unnatural but exceeding the normal laws of time, space, and causality. In Acts it is recorded:

> The many signs and wonders worked through the apostles made an awesome impression on everyone (Acts 2:45).

> Many signs and wonders were worked among the people by the hands of the apostles (Acts 5:12).

Throughout the scriptures there are numerous passages describing awesome signs such as healings, prophecy, resuscitation to life, clairvoyance, transmutation of matter, levitation, and others. Actually, the biblical text uses three words for miracles: *dunamis*, *semeion*, and *teras*. These Greek words may be translated respectively as "dynamic power," "signs or significant acts," and "a marvel or something that stirs excitement." The latter meaning always appears in the text with *semeion*, as in "signs and wonders." Paul writes:

> You have seen done among you all the things that mark the true apostle, unfailingly produced: the signs, the marvels, the miracles (2 Cor 12:12).

The thirteenth apostle is merely calling attention to what Jesus had already counseled his disciples about—their duplicating his wondrous deeds, even surpassing the Son of Man. The Bible, of course, does not narrate the entire careers of the disciples, let alone of Jesus. The connection between the performance of miracles and association with Jesus the master enabled these disciples to manifest similar powers over nature.

THE RELATIONSHIP BETWEEN BODY, MIND AND NATURE

The biblical accounts of this disciple relationship and the connection to miraculous powers are paralleled in the yoga tradition, which at this point can shed light on their explanation.

Human consciousness has the inner capacity to observe its functionings at work. By a simple inner reflection, one can watch one's own interior mental operations. From fragmentary ideas and impressions to complex concepts, one can witness one's mind endlessly absorbing and shaping its mental interior. In yoga psychology the mind-stuff which undergoes continual modifications is called *chitta*. When this mind-stuff assumes a shape (*chitta* taking form), then the modification of *chitta* is called a *vritti*. By the increased ability to assume control over the mental faculties and their expressions, one can discover the hidden potentials of consciousness.[7]

Strange as it may seem, yoga philosophy considers the mind and all its fluctuations as belonging to the realm of material being. Thinking, judging, desiring or remembering—even the slightest fluctuation or mental act—are considered vibrations of matter. Thus mind, as well as body, remains subject to the natural laws of material being. Biofeedback research would support this insight. Certainly the body differs from the mind, but this distinction is only relative, for there exists an organismic communion between them. Mind and body together share existence at the level of nature. Both are possessed by and subject to the field of material being. Yoga refers to this universal field of mass and energy as *prakrti*.

Nature does not resist man's effort to know it. On the contrary, nature, or *prakrti* (the realm of material being), has an affinity towards one's act of awareness; otherwise, the world would not be knowable. Energy, in other words, is at the service of consciousness.[8]

The conscious life center in one is called the *purusha*, the innermost knowing self, being akin to the Christian notion of soul as a life principle.[9] By invoking the law of self-concentration, one can extend the mind's influence over the body. One notices, for example, that exercising the body with attention produces agility. The awkwardness between mind and body ceases. Increasing awareness of the body makes the body more amenable to the mind's intention.

An art of awareness whereby both the mind and the body are brought under self-control is called meditation. The practice of meditation can extend mental control to encompass the mind and body's subtle areas, including the autonomic nervous system and the entire subconscious.[10]

When the yogi improves the meditation by developing a one-pointedness or *samyama* upon some aspect of matter, the focal point of interest comes under full control.[11] The entire intelligibility of the object of concentration is within one's grasp. Comprehending something in this manner is not an intellectual exercise like learning the rudiments of geometry or how to program software. Hardly. In focusing its penetrative power, consciousness apprehends not only the obvious sensual and intellectual arrangements of an object, those cognitive aspects available to rational knowing, but the entire range of its potentialities, including its history and destiny. *Samyama* means the mind assimilates an exhaustive inventory. All the knowable potentials, actual or latent, of its nature can be thoroughly comprehended.

The laws of meditation expand consciousness, as it were, to cover or pervade *prakrti* at will. Intuition and control go together; to know is to control from within. The mind does not impose its dominance from the outside, the way one's hand moves the steering wheel of an auto. Rather, the dexterity any healthy person displays with one's limbs, the yogi can perform with all bodies of matter.

Perfect intuition yields perfect control. Through the liberating practices of self-control, the accomplished yogi can consciously identify with matter freely, as though it were part of the self, and thus manipulate it.

Before gaining the ability to control nature, however, the yogi must acquire control over the individual *prakrti*. One's bodily nature incessantly makes demands upon the person. Unless the resonance of these appetites is understood and trained, one remains at the whim of their unpredictable reactions.

Up to this point the disturbing features of *prakrti* produced by the agitated mind and body have prevented the yogi from realizing comprehensive awareness. The physical conditions of ill health, improper diet, an imbalanced lifestyle, anxieties, and similar problems prevent the necessary interior pacification demanded for awareness to reach its intuitional levels. Unless an adept properly trains oneself in relation to one's own *prakrti*, nature keeps her secrets hidden.

A certain pacification through meditation is the key. When the mind-body ensemble is calmed, a spontaneous unity emerges that gradually allows more and better control over bodily *prakrti*. The self or spirit slowly recovers a self-conscious autonomy over its resident matter. The spirit loosens its stressful connections with *prakrti*. By developing a strong, tranquil integration of body, emotions, and thought processes, the natural correlation between spirit and matter occurs. The bodily impulses, the emotional flarings, the dissipation of the nervous system, all recede into a calmness that frees the mind from preoccupation with these lesser aspects of human nature. No longer restricted to their stressful demands, but fully respecting them when need be, the adept heightens his/her awareness to more subtle ranges of energy within and without. Nature has been the object of rational cognition; in addition, it now becomes the object of intuitional awareness. In rational knowing, the object is only thought about from the outside; now the object is known from its inner essence. The object's past, present, and future determinations are completely knowable and sublimated into the yogi's awareness.

Spiritual development always starts with the individual focusing upon personal growth in self-understanding. When spiritual growth proceeds through tranquil self-control, nature or *prakrti* reveals herself as one substantial field capable of unlimited modifications. A person's individual mind and body are only relatively distinct energy configurations within this field. Reason, of course, in its discursive mode of apprehending the external world, certifies otherwise. It views the world as separated, individual substances.

The yogi, however, from the superior vantage of meditative awareness, notices that every mental activity is an expression of *prakrti*. The apparent individuality is fundamentally a temporary differentiation of nature itself. Since the yogi's body and mind are a microcosm of the field of *prakrti*, they contain all the essential principles and factors found anywhere in nature. By deepening interior calmness, the yogi gains a full intuition of the nature of *prakrti*. Already liberated from the disturbances of body, mind, and external circumstances, the yogi now converts his or her awareness into perfect control of *prakrti* in all its aspects. Having purified self from egotism and other bondages, the yogi is spiritually seasoned and prepared to accept responsibility for the secrets of the cosmos. Nature will now acquiesce to the yogi's will. The realm of the miraculous is now available.

THE YOGA ACCOUNT OF MIRACLES

In the language of yoga, miracles are known as *siddhis*. The *Sutras* describe in chapter three many of the various feats that Christian theologians would classify as miraculous. The *Sutra* texts include methods for achieving clairvoyance, healing power, invisibility, reading minds, bilocation, multiplying food, levitation, and other phenomena that exactly parallel the wonders of the New Testament. These abilities emerge as part of the natural development of spirituality.

In examining the biblical accounts of miraculous events with an understanding of the relationship between consciousness and *prakrti*, the performance of a miracle—or the demonstration of a *siddhi*—corresponds proportionally to the state of spiritual integrity. In this way, universal laws of spiritual development provide for protection against their abuse. Before one can manifest truly supernatural or miraculous powers, there are certain personal requirements demanded of the individual. Usually these qualifications are prompted and groomed by a disciple under the tutelage of someone already spiritually advanced. The disciple-teacher relationship described in the gospels is not unique to the Semitic world, but is indigenous to the East. Once a reader is familiar with this common spiritual training method, then these gospel stories easily fit into place.

The progress of the disciple is closely observed by the teacher since the latter accepts a lifelong responsibility to assist the beloved students to their ultimate destiny. In their progress toward spiritual integration, the students' self-understanding grows and the abilities known as miraculous powers quite unassumingly emerge. Certain specific practices may be involved which can accelerate or refine these emerging capacities .

In rare instances some lesser powers, called psychic abilities, may suddenly manifest from the subconscious without the prescribed spiritual development. These instances may be detrimental to the true spiritual seeker. Others, however, misunderstand these occurrences in themselves and promote their own vanity and financial possibilities, thus turning a natural power into a spiritual deficit.

When ethical and psychological maturity is present in the disciple, the performance of these miracles or *siddhis* is not undertaken for self-aggrandizement. An examination of Jesus' performance reveals a serious attitude in every one of his miracles. There is never any effort to "show off" or tease the crowd into admiring him. The absence of egotistical motivations is apparent, and from a close analysis of the character of Jesus and other great sages one can obtain insight into the personal characteristics demanded of those who would call upon nature to obey them.

It may come more as a shock than a surprise for many Christians to learn that for centuries, even before Jesus' time, the performance of miraculous events has been a natural expression of a yogi's development. This is not to say that yogis occupy their time displaying miraculous powers. They are as discriminating as Jesus was in using his powers. There is abundant evidence that Jesus' miracles have been duplicated by yogis as well as other spiritual traditions throughout the world. The Old Testament likewise records similar miraculous events as found among Jesus and his disciples.

It is not difficult to compare a list of gospel miracles with the recorded *siddhis* of revered yogis. In this century alone, the lives of Rama Tirtha,

Aurobindo, Anandamayi Ma, Ramana Maharishi and others demonstrate the same miraculous performances as narrated in the New Testament.

Ananadamayi Ma, an Indian saint who left her body in 1982, showed her compassion toward those afflicted by healing them with a word or a touch. An episode is related in which one of her students was suffering from a severe crippling of the spine. When the student related his plight, Ma simply passed her hand over his spine and the pain vanished permanently. Another incident reminds one of Jesus' transfiguration. Ma began meditating with a group and announced that they should keep their eyes closed. Later, when they opened their eyes, they found a man lying unconscious in the hallway. Revived, he related that he came late and peeped into the room. He saw such an intense light radiating from Ma's face that he was unable to look at it for long and lost consciousness due to its overwhelming energy.[12]

Neem Karoli Baba, a modern yogi of northern India, had the *siddhi* of *annapurna* and was able to multiply food for his devotees as Christ did for the multitudes. An unusual intervention occurred when a student remarked how it was impossible for him to become a physician since he was a second-rate student and could not gain admittance to medical school. Baba simply touched the young man's head. Shortly thereafter the man was admitted to medical school and distinguished himself academically.[13]

Sri Swami Rama of the Himalayas tells the story of how he and his master were traversing a steep mountain path when an avalanche started above them. Being in its direct path they seemed doomed. The master just raised his hand, stopping the avalanche in mid air. When they reached the other side of the path, he waved his hand and the avalanche continued down the mountain side.[14]

There are countless other stories about yogis and saints that exactly resemble the episodes in the gospels. The yogi views the miracle or *siddhi* as the natural outcome of spiritual development. In fact, many of these *siddhis* come early in the path of spirituality before the aspirant has refined himself into a saint. The miraculous is not a power bestowed upon someone by an external agent—God or otherwise—but a natural unfoldment of latent abilities within human consciousness. These inherent powers are therefore not properly understood by evaluating them as performances of a divine agent intervening with natural laws.

Until modern science attained acceptance as a contributing factor in Western society, people often attributed the causal explanations for natural phenomena to divine intervention. Hence superstition abounded in the European mind. It took centuries before people realized that attributing the causal factors of natural events to God's intervening action does not truly explain the facts. The strong religious faith of the Middle Ages and the post-reformational centuries plus the limited understanding of the laws of nature combined to produce a static religious interpretation of the world, which for the most part endorsed God rather than alternative, natural explanations. Penalties were even affixed to unorthodox theories. Whenever science touched upon an interpretation that was considered the domain of religion, such as in cosmological theories, the essence of humankind and its faculties, creation and evolution, to name but a few, censorial treatment often ensued.

Three tragic episodes involve the scientists Giordano Bruno, who was burned at the stake by the ecclesiastical authorities, and Galilee Galileo, who was forced to recant his theories before the Christian inquisition and was placed under house arrest for the rest of his life. Throughout the centuries many of the theories of these men, and others like them, were accepted as orthodox science, due to the growing power and independence of scientific research. Surprisingly, it was not until 1984 that the Roman Church admitted its error with the Galileo case. The third tragic episode involves the witch burnings, the murder of thousands of women by male Christian authorities because these women dared to practice the art of healing.

The search for truth about reality may seem disruptive of the established worldview, but sometimes the advance of truth cannot avoid exposing the incompleteness of the current state of affairs.

The climate is hardly changing today. Science and religion grudgingly respect each other's realms and attempt to accommodate themselves to their own limitations. However, this separation of science and religion may be too severe. Some religious authorities feel that scientific propositions can aid in the understanding of religious truths. Bultmann, for example, is correct in his insistence that miracles meet the criticism of scientific investigation. Unfortunately, he carries this norm too far by denying any scientific respectability to these phenomena. Because he is unfamiliar with the evidence that yoga research provides, which illustrates that "miracles" are based on profoundly subtle but natural laws, he presumes that the gospel accounts are not to be taken in any objective sense.

On the other hand, Barth, who respects the biblical text as well as the domain of science, is reluctant to dismiss the gospel wonders as merely religious poetry. His insistence that the miraculous phenomena occurred only during the apostolic era reveals an ultraconservative judgment about modern people's possibilities for miracles, as well as a narrow understanding of natural laws.

Both scholars revere the gospel accounts and want to interpret them for twentieth-century humanity. Neither one, however, is able to render a satisfactory explanation for the presence of miracles in history, let alone the accumulating evidence today that demonstrates that one's abilities far exceed what theologians and scientists of the of this century thought possible.

Likewise, other theologians are aware of the research in biofeedback, mind-body medicine, and parapsychology, but have neglected to incorporate these findings into their understanding of the range of human possibilities. They, too, assume a too diminutive view of human nature. The scientific data in various institutes in North America and Europe that explore the nature of consciousness and its control over bodily functions and material energy are forcing new implications in the area of human nature for both science and religion.[15]

Barth, Bultmann, and other theologians remain too incomplete in their basic analysis of human nature. They share this limitation with all Christian churches. Confronted with the deficiencies and accomplishments of ordinary people, they allow this behavior to be their prototype of human nature. In contrast with the normal portrait of human beings, they juxtapose Jesus Christ. Although Jesus manifested the same basic nature as others of the human race, the quality of his human expression sets him apart radically. No one would doubt his human competence. But whether theologians are justified in maintaining that Jesus' level of humanness is inaccessible to the rest of humanity, thereby indicating some essentially different kind of living being requires more evidence than is generally found in theological manuals or scriptures.

Biblical texts state explicitly, and on more than one occasion, that Jesus' followers would be able to duplicate his wondrous feats—even supersede them. The description in the book of Acts narrates the astonishment of the citizens at the wonders and powers demonstrated by the disciples. Barth is quite reasonable in supposing that these divine gifts were necessary in order for people to realize the caliber of the Christian way. The question here, then, is why Barth and so many biblical scholars suddenly halt at this point, declaring what amounts to a moratorium on miracles? Bultmann in his accommodation to modern culture shows a profound ignorance, like so many theologicans in their cartesian dichotomy of spirit and matter, about the inherent psycho-somatic potentialities of human nature. The uneven history of saints and mystics belies this hesitancy on the part of religious scholarship. Holy men and women have abundantly expressed similar gifts or spiritual accomplishments in their recorded careers. Before and after the apostolic period, within Christianized cultures and elsewhere, a brief survey of religions and non-Christian spiritualities easily supports the identical array of miracles or *siddhis* that only prejudice would attribute to one version of religion.

To pose a scientific spirituality would not endanger the authenticity of divine truths embodied in a religion. On the contrary, a dialogue between yoga, science, and organized religion would help clear the air of reactionary suspicions and provide the background for a corrective appreciation of the mystery of Christ as well as the inherent dignity of human beings.

CHRISTIAN GNOSTICISM AND YOGA

Near the pharaonic tombs of the sixth dynasty, half-way up the Nile towards Cairo, a remarkable discovery took place in 1945. This incident was hardly known outside the Middle East since the rest of the world was busy celebrating the end of World War II.

Searching for fertilizer, a camel driver found a large jar, one meter high, hidden in a cave. Cracking the vessel open, he watched a bundle of papyrus texts spill to the ground. At this point, various versions of the discovery are expounded. One account relates how the peasant hid his find in a corner of his house and ran to inform the authorities only to find the treasure being used by his mother to start the evening fire at his return. Another version has him selling the cache for three Egyptian pounds to an antique dealer.

Veiled with obscurity, there now begins a long trail of intrigue, vanity, and professional competition among archeologists, governments, museums, and translators that delayed the discovery from reaching the English-speaking world for nearly half a century. The earthen jar had yielded fifty-one various manuscripts, forty-one of which were completely unknown to the amazed scholars. Fragments of letters and receipts used to reinforce the bindings bore dates to 333 A.D. Here was the most extensive documentation yet of the early Christian sect known as the Gnostics.

These writings are collectively known as the *Nag Hammadi Library*, borrowed from the name of the small town near the spot of discovery, or the *Chenobaskion Manuscripts*, from a Christian monastery in the same neighborhood. More extensive than the Dead Sea Scrolls discovered in 1941, these writings shed a rich and surprising light upon one of the most controversial periods of early Christianity. While not receiving notoriety outside academic circles, the contents of the *Nag Hammadi Library* may shock Christians who read them.

Most Christians take it for granted that the New Testament contains only four Gospels, some letters, and the Book of Revelations. Yet the *Nag Hammaldi Library* reveals the gospels of Mary, Thomas, Philip, Truth, and The Egyptians. There are the additional Revelations of James, Paul, Adam, and Peter. Since the compilation of any gospel occurred over a period of many years, it is not unusual that there could be more than the conventional four of the New Testament. What is perhaps the most surprising is the addition of strange new texts: Thunder, the Perfect Mind; the Second Word of the Great Seth; The Testimony of Truth; and The Dialogue of the Redeemer, to name but a few.

From a careful analysis of the *Nag Hammadi Library*, three inferences are drawn. First, while duplicating the gospel stories, the newly discovered manuscripts expand further the life of Jesus and his followers, often leading the reader to interpretations different from those upheld by mainline Christian churches.

Second, the *Nag Hammadi Library* shows that there are many spiritual traditions, from the Greek to the Oriental, comprising the essence of Gnosticism. The texts called Teaching of Truth of Zostrianos, the God of Truth, and The Song of the Pearl would indicate, for example, the Persian tradition associated with the religion of Zoroastrianism.

Third, the *Nag Hammadi Library* shows that there was an inter-relationship between Gnosis and conventional Christianity as well as their independence from each other. A Christianizing of Gnosis and a Gnosticizing of Christianity occurred. Even the Church Fathers, the more orthodox theologians of the early Church, spoke of their true gnosis over and against the Gnostics' versions.

It is important never to lose sight of the historical fact that the Gnostics were not alien to the Christians, nor viewing themselves as an opposing religious sect, but in reality were mostly Christians who upheld beliefs which they considered genuinely Christian. St. Paul himself expounds many ideas that are compatible and apparently identical with the Gnostic interpretation of Jesus and the church. It is evident that there are instances in Paul's epistles when he opposed them, yet there are more instances when he is completely in accord with them. In his letter to the Ephesians, for example, Paul portrays Jesus as the cosmic man (Ephesians 1:10) which is a Gnostic concept. His notion that flesh and spirit are irreconcilable (Romans 8:5-10; 13:11-13), as well as the idea that the spiritual Christ is decisive and not the earthly one (2 Corinthians 5:16) are likewise Gnostic ideas. One can only speculate to what extent Paul's decision to use Gnostic ideas and terms came from his spiritual experience and/or his reflections in finding them appropriate. That he used them is clearly evident.

THE MEANING OF GNOSIS

The Greek word *gnosis* means "knowledge or understanding." Its use in designating sects of Christians in the first to the fifth centuries carries the nuance of a special type of knowledge. Unlike faith or intellectual knowledge, gnosis meant an esoteric or intuitive understanding that is inaccessible to rational analysis. In this sense gnosis is more akin to the *para vidya* of the *Upanishads*, a higher knowledge available only to the trained ordinary mind which the yogis seek in higher states of consciousness called *samadhi*. This special knowledge revealed the ultimate meaning of life and the universe.

> If anyone has gnosis, he is a being who comes from above....He knows like someone who was drunk and has become sober from his drunkenness and, restored again to himself, has again set his own in order (Gospel of Truth).[1]

In fact, the Gnostics ridicule denominational faith. In their eyes faith has at best a provisional role and can never be a substantial way to salvation. It is too narrow a premise going nowhere since it is empty of result, having only pious allegations. This unyielding stance conflicted with the orthodox bishops' emphasis on the exclusive role of faith. That the Gnostics resisted any authoritative clergy in their ranks did not help their relations with the Christian Church. The Gnostic heritage dwelled upon those religious themes that would occupy the minds of any Christian: God, the world, and human nature. Yet there was no emphasis upon a normative theology, no rule of faith or insistence upon the importance of an external dogma. This de-emphasis upon strict credentials of faith would be consistent with a movement that concerned itself more with an interior realization of these ideas than outward conformity. From an investigation of the Nag Hammadi texts, the Gnostics allowed a very diversified presentation of what one may broadly refer to as the Gnostic theology. Apparently this toleration for varying viewpoints carried over in their communities where there was a wide range of conduct from the bizarrely ritualistic to the purely internalized ascetic.

Historically, the Gnostics never encouraged theological conformity. Their concepts of God, human nature, and the universe were considered so radical by the more conventional Christians that a large number of orthodox theologians wrote against them. Men like Justin (165 A.D.), Irenaeus (180 A.D.), Tertullian (200 A.D.), Hyppolytus (225 A.D.), Clement (200 A.D.), and Origin (250 A.D.) tried to expose the intellectual and moral dangers in the Gnostic camp. These authors, it is to be remembered, wrote against the Gnostics from a siege mentality, as it were, struggling to combat ideas and practices that they thought would seriously endanger the salvation of souls. Valuable as their polemical writings are, it is not unlikely that many quotations from the Gnostics were pulled out of context and passionate accusations took the place of fair critical analysis.

These tensions are all the more interesting in that the Gnostics produced the first and largest theological literature among Christian writings. The intensity of the polemic was during the second and third centuries. Afterwards the movement ebbed, probably due to the consolidation of Christianity under Emperor Constantine in 313 A.D. and the persistent pressure banning the independent Gnostic ideas and writings.

THE SCOPE OF GNOSIS

The Gnostic texts reveal a rich heritage of contributory sources and original reflection. Indo-Persian, Jewish, Greek, Egyptian, and Christian concepts fill out the mosaic of its teachings. If one can leave aside, for the moment, the judgment of the Catholic bishops and theologians that saw Gnostic Christians misled at best, and the progeny of Satan at worst, then the major features of these writings provoke new questions even for our present day.

From the material of the *Nag Hammadi Library*, one sees that several divergent versions of the same theme are found side by side. Apparently, the Gnostic communities appreciated the manifold ways that a text could be interpreted. This method of taking an ancient text and rendering different implications from it was not so much an instance of subjectivism as an illustration of the untold depth of a tradition that required a varied approach in order to extract the fullness of meaning. This method of explication is found throughout the East. The *Yoga Sutras* and the *Bhagavad Gita*, for example, have had many commentaries written about them over the centuries. What makes the *Nag Hammadi* discovery so interesting to scholars and readers is that the divergent views are all assembled together. Again, it must not be overlooked that the four conventional gospels of the New Testament are not four successive chapters composing a single description of Jesus and his period. On the contrary, these gospels provide four distinct portraits, similar to each other and yet individually interpreted to depict meaning that the others may or may not evidence. The narration of Jesus' birth in Matthew is radically different from the account in Luke; at face value they seem contradictory to each other.

The Gnostic writings show an ability to express ideas in ever new ways, borrowing from previous traditions at times, and reframing the older mythological material for their purposes. The essential features of the Gnostic myth are readily available throughout the divergent texts. It is to these fundamental conceptions that this chapter pertains.

THE GNOSTIC COSMOS

The description of the universe—the Gnostic cosmology—was not invented afresh. The Gnostic teachers inherited a worldview typical to both semite and Christian. It was the Ptolemaic world with the earth at the center surrounded by air and eight heavenly spheres. These spheres contain the seven planets and the fixed stars. Beyond or above this geocentric astronomy is the realm of the unknown God residing in the *pleroma* or graduated worlds of "fullness." These two realms—the eternal world of God the Father—and the heavenly hierarchy and the vast created world—are irreconcilable. The planetary spheres enclose "demons" or "rulers" that can exert unruly influence upon men. The chief ruler is the *Demiurgos*, the creator God who produced the phenomenal realm. Together this God and the invisible demons constitute the kingdom of "fate" for man. The treacherous cosmos is variously referred to as darkness, deception, and death. These cosmic powers dominate the human condition through the signs of the zodiac.

The tyranny of the stars is unique to the Gnostics. While the Asiatic and Greek cosmologies found fault with the world, none of them equated matter with evil as did the Gnostics. The yogis who recognize the *Vedanta* philosophy may agree with the Gnostics about the deficiency and illusion of the universe, but would hardly declare it incorrigibly hostile. For the Gnostics the entire manifested world offered not the slightest pause from the relentless kingdom of darkness. How did the cosmos get this way? The Gospel of Philip states:

> The world came into being through a transgression. For he
> who created it wanted to create it imperishable and immortal.
> He failed and did not attain to his hope.[2]

The natural world is an alluring mistake. While there are differences over the number of hostile powers, the Gnostics hold that mankind is induced by sinister spirits of all types to forget his higher nature and be subject to their unholy ends.

The complexities of the cosmic schema differ in various texts but the essential negative stance is the same. No wonder, then, that the neo-Platonists, the Roman Stoics and the Church Fathers line up vigorously against the Gnostics. For in the eyes of these opponents, the cosmos was essentially sound, ruled by a beneficent creator, inspiring humanity by its beauty and order to pursue its divine origin. Similarly, in the *Vedas* there are innumerable endorsements of the glory of the universe. It is from this positive beauty that the yogis draw their inspiration for transcendence.

> Even as the radiance of the sun enlightens all regions, above, below, and slantwise, so that only God, glorious and worthy of worship, rules over all his creation.[3]

HUMAN NATURE AND DESTINY

Just as the sensual body and rational mind have an affinity for the world and its enticing snares, so with everyone there is an inner person possessing an eternal spark of light, according to Gnostic belief. This light is divine, the very essence of the person. St. Paul mentions the same concept in his letter to the Roman community reminding his followers to "cast off the works of darkness and put on the armor of light" (Romans 13:12).

Gnostic anthropology portrays a threefold composition of human nature. There is the flesh or body, the psychic or mind, and the self or soul. The personality of each individual is determined by which of the three elements— body, mind, or spirit—predominates. The person of flesh is a captive to the world of illusion and transience. Enslaved of the devil, that soul is blind and deaf even to the need for salvation. The body is described as a robe or coat covering the mental dimension, attracted to the alluring mire of creation. One's capitulation to the vagaries of matter only increases the forgetfulness of one's original true nature. Humans are at war with themselves and the evil spirits, feeling at times a longing for a higher life but immediately opposed by mundane desires and passions which direct their energies otherwise. The biblical symbol indicating this personality is Cain.

The personality of the psychic or mental individual shows itself by developing rational capacities. Such a person stands in the middle between the carnal and the spiritual. S/he must choose a personal destiny, either aspiring to Gnosis or perishing in sensual mortality.

The pneumatic personality, the person of spirit, is aware of the relationship to God. In fact, the gradual self-knowledge brings the insight that one is a divine person. The Gnostic readily endorsed the Psalm verse, "You are gods, all sons of the most high" (Psalms 82:6). The biblical type for this personality is Seth.

In recognizing a divine core within, the Gnostics submitted a new metaphysical status in the order of existence: humans are above the creator God, the *Demiurgos*. It is a human's kinship with the unknown God, the Father/Mother God, which, once awakened, enables one to return to the real kingdom and renounce the worthless world as one's destiny.

Few people, however, will achieve the spiritual status of the elect or perfect ones who allow the light within to burn brightly forever. The reason for the paucity of members has been foretold in Genesis. The Adam and Eve story in various manuscripts reveal the human descent into matter and the struggle that everyone goes through. This biblical story is the prototype for the human condition, showing the need for redemption.

THE NOTION OF SALVATION

Humans need salvation from the world. Redemption, resurrection, and gnosis are equivalently understood as salvation. Instead of considering resurrection as a corporeal reuniting of a body with the soul after death— the conventional Christian appraisal—the Gnostics offered a complex assessment. Resurrection combined first the inflaming of the soul's spark of light. This resuscitation came through the call of a redeemer and especially through self-knowledge. In this way the ignorance of forgetfulness is overcome. Secondly, the liberated spirit ascends to the heavenly kingdom, the *pleroma*.

In some texts this spiritual consummation takes place at physical death while others insist it must occur before death. In the flexible presentation of the texts, perhaps it would be better to posit resurrection on two levels: one, a self-transformation in consciousness wherein the individual's experience of gnosis is like a rebirth or resurrection, (the word resurrection in Greek conveys the notions of a re-awakening as well as a raising) and two, a final release from the corporeal dimension signified by death's irretrievable separation of spirit from matter. Here one finds an inconsistency with the

Gnostic stand on matter. Some of the texts allow for the existence of a new body after death; a spiritual flesh ensues that acts as a bearer of the spirit. Apparently for some, the body was not as abhorrent as previously claimed.

At the same time, individual resurrection depicts a later total consummation of the universe at the end of time. All souls will be properly disposed. Some, the elite, will enjoy eternal beatitude; others, not so lucky, will face eternal perdition. A world cyclic process is absent from the texts, for the cosmos will meet a final dissolution. In the meantime, the psychic or mental personalities will undergo reincarnation for a few times in hope that they will finally choose *gnosis*.

DUALISM AND THE ROLE OF A REDEEMER

Gnosis embraces a dualism, metaphysical in scope, which divides the unknown god and the inner man or woman on one side away from the creator-ruler God with his demonic army and the material universe. Being matter and spirit, a human is a microcosm reflecting the vast struggle between ignorance and knowledge, evil and good, perdition and enlightenment. The removal of ignorance, the barrier to salvation, is the process of *gnosis*. The Gospel of Philip states:

> Ignorance is a slave. Knowledge is freedom. When we recognize
> the truth we shall find the fruits of the truth in us. If we unite
> with it, it will bring our fulfillment.[4]

Unlike the comprehensive approach of yoga, Gnosticism has no insistence of an integration of body, mind, and spirit for genuine freedom. Yet the Gnostics do not posit liberation as an automatic event with no preparation. In many texts there is an emphasis upon ethical behavior and ascetical practices to reinforce and preserve the elite state. Undoubtedly, gnostic liberation is basically self-redemption. The idea of a redeemer corresponds more to the role of an inspiring paradigm, someone who has demonstrated the possibility of freedom from the cosmos. This is quite similar to the role of *avatars*, or divine incarnations, in Eastern thought.

The Gnostic texts, as expected, do not present a uniform necessity for a redeemer. For some, the redeemer is an emissary of light shining forth in the earthly darkness, a beacon of truth that illuminates the way. For others, the figure of Jesus has been mythologized into a central role. While the exclusive reliance upon redemption through a redeemer, as found in orthodox circles, is foreign to the Gnostic mind, the representation of Jesus Christ at times assumes a special status: Jesus is the revealer and prophet of Gnostic wisdom. In the form of secret traditions, Jesus imparts this wisdom to his elect, often through the mediation of privileged disciples, such as Peter, James, John, and Thomas. He is the light person, the personification of God. His incarnation into time and space entails him to enter hell and confront the psychic demons that pervade the universe. Peter (1 Peter 5:19) and Paul (Ephesians 4:9) stated the same.

Some Gnostic manuscripts are quite similar to the gospels' version of Jesus. A comparison of St. John's Gospel with the Gnostic's Gospel of Truth reveals a compatibility of description regarding Jesus and his resurrected body that would deny any division of orthodox belief and heretical opinion. Yet the portrait of Jesus as the Christ is complicated and variously proposed in other texts. The Apocalypse of James mentions a conversation between the resurrected Jesus and the grieving apostle James:

> Never have I experienced any kind of suffering, nor was I tormented...[5]

In the Second Word of Seth, it is mentioned of Jesus:

> I did not suffer at all. They sought to punish me and I died, not in reality but only in appearance. [6]

The Gnostic viewpoint sees Jesus as not truly suffering but yet giving the appearance that the torture and crucifixion were producing pain. In the Revelation of Peter, the savior states:

> He whom you see on the wood glad and laughing, this is the living Jesus. But he in whose hands and feet they drive nails

is his fleshly likeness, it is the substitute....Accordingly only that which is capable of suffering will suffer, in that the body is the substitute. He however who was set free is my bodiless body; for I am only perceptible spirit which is full of radiant light...[7]

For the Gnostics, victory over the flesh means that Jesus transcended any pain. In so doing, he proves the liberation of the spirit over matter and its deficiencies. There is a curious story of St. Teresa of Avila that relates how once the convent nuns found her rapt in meditation and attempted to revive her by sticking her with pins, to no avail. Likewise there are ancient techniques taught to yogis that enable them to supersede sensible pain while remaining conscious of their environment.

THE UNKNOWN GOD

The ultimate Lord of Being is the unknown God. This God did not create anything. The Gnostic concept of God is similar to the Eastern notion of *Brahman*. There are no images or ideas that can in any way describe this super-transcendental God. Genderless, absolutely real, but incomprehensible to the rational mind. By contrast with sense and reason, God is unknown, yet the Father and Mother of the All, the beginning and end of everything. Strange that the best description of God is in negative terms. What God is not is also the exact portrayal of God by Jewish and Christian theologians and mystics. Thomas Aquinas, Meister Eckhart, the author of *The Cloud of Unknowing*, John of the Cross, are but a few authors whose experience, like that of many Eastern sages, concurs with the Gnostic description. The revelation of gnosis eventually overcomes their fundamental ignorance.

The notion of addressing God as Father existed side by side with revering God as divine Mother. In the Gospel to the Hebrews, Jesus speaks of "my Mother, the Spirit."[8] The same is reiterated in the Gospel of Thomas and the Gospel of Philip. There are many other manuscripts that describe the divinity as feminine. Interestingly, in the manuscript called *The Triple-Formed Primal Thought*, the range of consciousness is predominantly identified as female and later asserts the androgynous dynamism of the human spirit. Here are echoes of tantra yoga with its description of consciousness comprised of the primal powers of *shakti* (female) and *siva* (male).

SUMMARY

The rediscovery of the hundreds of manuscripts that make up the *Nag Hammadi Library* have yet to be fully appreciated for their value as a form of Christianity and as a synthesis of spiritual traditions. The following reflections may be offered about them.

1. The context of the manuscripts is myth. There is no fixed dogma. The preference for myth allows for an absorption of various strands of diverse traditions that can explain the message. The wide differences and emphasis on just what is appropriate for each group of Gnostics can be tolerated within the multifaceted symbols comprising Gnostic mythology.
2. The Gnostics resisted idolizing any special teacher. The few Gnostic authors may have inspired followers but there is little evidence pointing to a cultic status for them as is found in other forms of Christianity around Jesus, Mary, and the saints.

Unlike institutional Christians, the Gnostics did not share in the third-century movement that associated divine power on earth with a limited number of human agents—apostles, martyrs, bishops, and saints. Hence they resisted becoming consolidated into a clergy with its attendant policies and privileges. Their approach obviously alienated them from the more orthodox church.
3. There is a radical unknowability regarding God. While this strong position is not entirely absent from the Jewish and Christian Bibles, it is rarely emphasized by orthodox theologians. The Gods and traditions derived from the cosmos are entirely rejected as worthless. This disdain for the material world is more than just a recognition of the limitations of earthly existence; it shows up in the manuscripts as a negative evaluation: matter is a perpetual enemy.
4. The emphasis upon self-redemption allows the Gnostics a wide diversity of beliefs is evident in the *Nag Hammadi Library*. The central emphasis is on the practical truth of achieving liberation now, not a speculation about the cosmos or a discussion of the fine points of doctrine. Neither will faith produce liberation. One must be conscious of the real truth, the *gnosis*. The

Gnostics saw themselves as the only true Christians. To be without gnosis is to remain in ignorance, like living in a nightmare. In the Dialogue of the Savior, when Jesus is asked to show Matthew the pure light and its place, Jesus replies, "Every one of you who has known himself has seen it."[9] Again in the Testimony of Truth we are told that one must become a "disciple of one's own mind."[10]

5. The worst evil that befalls people is self-ignorance, like a disease; the only cure is self-knowledge. In this Gnostic light, the gospels become favorable to the yoga insistence that self-knowledge is liberating. The Gnostic teacher Silvanus says: "Light the lamp within you."[11] The Gospel of Thomas likewise asserts: "When you come to know yourselves, then you will be known and you will realize that you are the sons of the living Father." [12]

In its complexity the Gnostic heritage offers to orthodox Christians the opportunity to reconsider the depth of spiritual experience available to seekers who follow Christ. As Christians ask questions about the meaning of life and inner experience that exceed the standard answers provided by institutional churches, the Gnostic writings, along with yogic practices, point to human horizons available for the exploration.

COMPANIONS FOR THE FUTURE

As we fathom our true nature and ultimate destiny we realize sooner or later that the world cannot measure up to our aspirations. Most of us eventually compromise on this assessment by plateauing too early in life while our unrestricted desire to fulfill our dreams smolders. The portrait of our lives thus leaves blank spots eventually filled in with the painful consequences of not knowing who we are.

By birth we are anonymous candidates for *religio perennis*, perennial religion, for while we cannot help but afix our energies to pursue ultimate realilty, we get confused as to how to direct the titanic life force within our hearts to its ultimate homeland. Urged from within and beckoned from without, our lifeforce shapes a career, establishes a family, gathers friends for a few score years to know, to love, and to express our freedom as best we can in material expressions. In our best moods we strive to resume our highest aspirations, sensing that there is more to life, a subtle call that can subsume our earthly career with an irresistible vision of transcendent possibilities. While our careers may stumble or fail, our inner thirst to fulfill and enjoy our life refuses to abate.

If we but gather up our successes and accomplishments, however minor, along with our punishing failures and missed opportunities, however major, we objectively demonstrate a transpersonal character, an imminent and transcendent capactiy to embrace the infinite. Our continual wrestling with life shows that the thirst for knowledge and the ardor to love knows no limits, except temporarily when our imagination falters and our body fatigues. Once refreshed we oblige, in varying degrees, this thrusting impulse to continue engaging life, come what may. Our spirit's refusal to back off from the challenges of life shows a vastly different career then the summation of our resume.

The human spirit is meant for ultimate truth, eternal existence, and unalloyed beauty. Living compels each of us to give vent to this threefold exigency. We feel it prompting all our sundry efforts to experience life and bring forth its manifestations. In all its marvelous diversity, the human race shares from its collective core an unremiting need to find and give expression to these highest impulses. While our everyday efforts seem so pitiful against what we sense could be achieved, these endeavors develop the virtues necessary to kindle the capacity for wisdom. Rightfully so, for the call to a divine life, unlike democracy, will not suffer compromise. Only an absolute reality can justify our implacable appetites. If not, then the call to live is in vain.

LOSS OF THE SENSE OF THE SACRED

Hindsight shows that the moment Jesus became clothed in Churchly garments, he became problematic. How else can one explain the complexities of at least four hundred versions of Christianity in the United States today? Which group best informs the world of who Jesus is, what he said, and what he stands for?

We can, nevertheless, delineate a common unity among these diverse believers. In Western society especially, Jesus Christ embodies the proto-human for Christians' innate desire for perfection. This is always, of course, filtered through a church affiliation. Christian belief in the resurrected Jesus is the centerpiece of *religio perennis*. His brief earthly career and continuing existence in a glorious afterlife has brought an inextinguishable light to the fundamental ignorance that confounds humankind's quest for ultimate meaning and illumines how the human aspiration for total fulfillment may be compensated. Jesus personifies the salvific gift of wisdom for humanity.

No doubt agreement may be reached on this general portrait of Jesus, but given the times we live in, there is a chasm full of confusion about life. This is not so much a confrontation with orthodoxy, but rather a larger disruption afflicting all human beings. A brief survey of Amnesty International's compilation of human conflicts in our times shows that more humans have been uprooted, tortured, enslaved, exiled, bankrupted, and destroyed amidst the political catastrophes of the twentieth century than in any period in recorded history. One could make a case that the destructive violence and recurring conflict are of such a magnitude that they issue from essential components of human nature that have apparently lain in wait until the ripe circumstances provided by this century.

In this distrusting climate inherited religious orthodoxy is unheeded by inhabitants who resent putting their confidence in any official authority. Intensifying the distrust, the scientific and industrial communities ensure a desacralization of nature. Instead of explaining a fascinating cosmos, physicists proclaim a purposeless universe—a wildly, random concatenation of unpredictable forces and atoms sporadically colliding to form a temporary galaxy. Biology offers the consolation of a haphazard, evolutionary past that replicated humans from mindless primates. Medical science treats patients as accidental aggregates of molecules subject to mechanical remedies, conveniently separating the patient's body from its mind and emotions. Business enterprises view market forces independently of moral considerations or ecological consequences.

In their unrelieved anxiety about living in what appears an unfriendly, irrational world, men and women question any natural connection with the transcendent aspects of the cosmos. The theological perspective, except in a most abstract, academic fashion, shrinks from seeing and celebrating creation as an intelligible and energizing manifestation of the divine. Nature and matter are effectively neutered from their sacred symbolism. Bereft of an invigorating cosmic order, we become inhabitants of a cold planet, subject to eventual entrophy. The conviction of living in an ordered wholeness, a cosmos transfused with divine imprints to insinuate a future vision where nature and transcendent reality form a unifying continuum for humanity to rediscover its primordial inheritance, is banished to a dimmed, irretrievable past. In desperation Christain pedagogy asserts blind leaps of faith to a distant God in order to endure this "vale of tears" and grasp at some semblance of sanity. In this chance-driven, mechanized world, we all forget our sense of the sacred.

THE COMMON TASK FOR CHRISTIANITY AND YOGA

Christianity can hardly compel allegiance on the proof of its historical longevity, for some believers feel estranged from institutional history. The paradox and drama amidst the superabundance provided by technology in our information age is that it reenforces a scepticism for achieving spiritual autonomy. Where do we start in the endless variety of New Age religions, various psycho-spiritual and occult movements all vying with the mainline churches and synagogues for the apparently lost soul of modern beings? Struggling in this unpredictable future, we attempt to assuage our core feelings of transience by cultivating "temporary relief." From fast-food, Rolaids and lotteries, to quick money schemes and politically-correct churches, the pace of life forces us to cleave to propaganda and anesthetize our painful disappointments rather than slow down to embrace the envigorating ordeal of living intelligently.

Strangely present amidst these scary ambiguities of existence, hopeful assertions and humane incidents grew across all cultural fronts. Shortly before World War I, the scientific world's worst nightmare showed up. The Newtonian myth of a totally mechanical, utterly deterministic universe, which fitted so nicely with the mindless notion of evolution, became embarrassed to explain the mounting evidence indicating that the dynamic forces of matter and energy were much more subtle, diverse, and different than ever suspected. Thus was born relativity theory and quantum physics. The energy of chaos was suspected of hiding new patterns of syntropic order yet to be discovered and utilized for human purposes. Similar emergents occured in medicine where, reluctantly, conventional, narrow approaches yielded to the more holistic protocals of Eastern and lesser known cultures which have always assumed that the human being is less a patient than a client, a conscious participant in the excursion to wellness.

The ghost of Descartes's body and mind separation is being exorcised by the investigations of body-mind medicine that show how thoughts become biology. A growing awareness of ecological responsibility challenges the indifferent attitude of business enterprise. In 1989 no one could have foretold the momentous events of Soviet Communism, the Berlin wall, and South Africa's Apartheid collapsing without the devastations of nuclear bombings or military invasions. Perhaps the irrational, chaotic display of nature and culture's discontinuities and disintegrations are natural and inevitable, allowing nature to catch her breath before reintegrating her energy pattern into new wholes. All this enhances life and reveals new opportunites for creative enterprises. Instead of a one-tiered world, we find that we live in a pluralistic cosmos where the Newtonian worldview becomes, not the scientific bible, but a contributory chapter in the encyclopedia of nature, most of which we have yet to read.

Perhaps, as the yoga sages mention, the human race, for all its dazzling accomplishments and profound injustices, continues to suffer from a profound ignorance of its ultimate identity. As long as humanity pursues its enterprises without acknowledging that it possesses a perfect, immortal essence, then it cannot escape its karmic consequences. Jesus reminded the crowds about sowing seeds and reaping the results. Searching here and there for completion, humanity's ersatz attempts to substitute anything less than the recognition of itself as the image of God—*Imago Dei*—eventually collapses into painful failure. The further we retreat from this acknowledgement and the action steps it entails, the greater and quicker the diasters befall our best efforts. Yet individuals throughout history, in all cultures, have pierced the veil of confusion and under the impact of a revelation have embodied and managed to broadcast to others the liberating significance of their theophonic experience.

Institutional Christianity may itself be still under the shadow of a Newtonian universe. That may be why it has such a hard time in truly appreciating the breadth of spiritual diversity. It continues to underestimate itself by not overhauling its language and conceptual approaches to present its religious vision. Its credentials of belief seem to be coercive allegations rather than inducements to discover the mystery of life.

The momentous task for Christianity and yoga is to restore the sacralization of nature on all its fronts. They have a task of reconstructing awareness of their primordial traditions and assessing integration with the present. For too long religions and philosophies have ignored their ecological responsibilities. How long can we practice faith or do yoga postures if we breathe polluted air, digest herbicide-riddled foods, and exhaust our nerves with stressful noise and hectic schedules? The enormous and unpredictable political and cultural changes since 1989 are a hopeful portent of even more humane changes that can occur if we are to pass on this world to our grandchildren.

While both traditions assume different starting points on life, neither would cancel out the other. The followers of Jesus have gathered together—*ecclesia*—and formed their beliefs into a religious tradition that affirms life here and hereafter. Yoga also proposes a philosophy of life, a genuine spirituality, that is in keeping with the highest values of humanity's religious impulse. Yoga's goal is twofold: the reduction of the roots of suffering and the promotion of health and spiritual well-being. For this it offers physical, emotional, mental and ethical tools. Together both traditions, each in their own way, trace their roots to a primordial source of sacred knowledge. Both traditions honor human beings as sacred. Both share ethical principles founded on love and truth. But whereas yoga emphasizes conscious experience, exoteric Christians hold belief as crucial, and while Christianity centers its devotion around the figure of Jesus Christ, yoga focuses on the personal attainment of the Christ Consciousness.

What yoga must do is bring its coherent vision into the marketplace to affect the well being of society. For Christian churches to succeed, they must be vigilant to the temptation of imperialism. The more authoritarian and doctrinaire a religion becomes, the more its zeal distorts spiritual growth. Those whose spirit is underdeveloped find in the ideals of authoritarian religion a collective strength which they as individuals admire but fail to achieve. In this respect, submission to an external system of beliefs either satisfies their dimly understood need for power and significnace, or gives them freedom from self-responsibility.

One of the fruitful ways for institional religion to protect itself from exclusion and commercial competition is to engage the vital core of other spiritual traditions: to meet and learn in dialogue. No radical pursuit of essential questions can be intelligently conducted without acknowledging the necessary co-existence of other traditions. This is not a surrender to theological relativism but the candid admission that absolutes are clothed in finite garb for human communication. Theological language, no matter how scrupulously composed, is a finite enterprise in time and space and thus cannot exhaust the intelligible meanings available for investigation.

Endorced by both Christianity and yoga, the sacredness of all life will then show its rainbow of expressions. The primal responsibility of Christianity and yoga is to lovingly bring about the expressions of truthful evidence that awaken the human spirit's center to its true gnosis, the *Sophia perennis*, that eternal wisdom that sleeps, expectantly, within.

NOTES

CHAPTER ONE: TRADITIONS IN TANDEM

1 Martyr, Justin. *Dialog with Trypho*. (Baltimore: Westminster Press), 1958, p. 75.

2 Archbishop Jean Jadot in *Bulletin: Secretariatus pro Non Christianis*, 1983, XVIII/1. 52, p. 22-23.

3 See Candace Pert, "The Chemical Communicators" in Bill Moyer's *Healing and the Mind*, (New York: Doubleday) 1993, p.177-193.

CHAPTER TWO: THE WAYS OF RELIGIOUS CONSCIOUSNESS

1 Van Ruysbrock, Jan. *The Spiritual Espousals*, edited and translated by E. Colledge, (London: Sheed and Ward), 1952, p. 187.

2 Meister Eckhart. *Sermon 99*. Quoted in Underhill, Mysticism, (New York: New American Library), 1955, p. 420.

3 *Theologia Germanica*, Ch. 41, quoted in Underhill, *op. cit.*, p. 418.

4 Underhill, *op. cit.*, p. 342.

5 *Ibid.*, p. 149.

6 Elmer, O'Brien. *Varieties of Mystic Experience*, (New York; New American Library), 1965, p. 77.

7 *Ibid.*, p. 79.

8 *Maitri Upanishad*, 6.17.

9 *Mandaka Upanishad*, 3.2.8.

10 *Svetasvatara Upanishad*, 2.15.

11 *Kaivalya Upanishad*, 7.

12 *Katha Upanishad*, 4.1.

13 *Ibid.*, 6.18.

14 Richard of St. Victor. *Selected Writings on Contemplation*, edited and translated by C. Kirchberger, (London: Sheed and Ward), 1957, p. 203.

15 St. Edmund Rich. "The Mirror" in: The Mediaevel Mystics of England, edited and translated by E. Colledge, (London: Sheed and Ward), 1961, p. 137-39.

16 Origin. *Commentary on John 32.27* in: Andrew Louth, *Christian Mystical Tradition from Plato to Denys*, (Oxford: Oxford University Press), 1983, p. 73.

17 Maslow, Abraham. *Religions, Values and Peak Experiences* , (New York: Viking Press), 1970, p. 24-25.

18 *Ibid.*, p. 25.

CHAPTER FIVE: YOGA AND THE JESUS PRAYER

1 Kodloubovsky. E. and Palmer, G.E. H. (trs.). *Writings from the Philokalia on Prayer of the Heart*, (London: Faber and Faber), 1951, p. 6.

[2] The riddle of why Western Christianity lost this treasure of spirituality may be traced in some measure to the door of St. Benedict. As the Father of Western Monasticism, he opened to his followers in Europe a path of spirituality based on the imitation of Christ as witnessed in his moral virtues. Without in any way minimizing the role of prayer or meditation in his rule, we see that there is not the slightest hint of the prayer of the heart nor any direction towards a psychophysical incorporation of these spiritual principles in his famous rule for the monastic life. As a monk of his time, Benedict was familiar with this ascetic approach, found both in the Rule of Basil, which he relied upon for the composition of his own rule, as well as the Conferences of Cassian (360-435 A.D.). No doubt the Hesychast method was known to him. Whatever his reasons, he preferred not to introduce it in his writings nor apparently to his order of monks.

[3] Kodloubovsky, E. and Palmer, G.E. H. *op. cit.*, p. 192.

[4] *Ibid.*, p. 192-93.

[5] *The Yoga Sutras of Patanjali*, 1. 2-3.

[6] Cuttat, Jacques-Albert. *The Encounter of Religions*, (New York: Desclie Company), 1960, p.102.

[7] *Ibid.*, p. 102.

[8] *Ibid.*, p. 103.

[9] *Ibid.*, p. 125.

[10] Kodloubovsky, E. and Palmer, G.E.H., *op. cit.*, p. 33.

[11] Cuttat, *op. cit.*, p. 99.

[12] Kodloubovsky, E. and Palmer, G.E.H., *op. cit.*, p. 235.

[13] Johnston, William (ed.), *The Cloud of Unknowing and the Book of the Privy Counseling* (anon) (New York: Doubleday Image Books), 1973, p. 149.

[14] Ruysbroeck, John. *The Adornment of the Spiritual Marriage.*, translated by P. Wynschenk Dom, (London: Faber & Faber), 1916, 1. ii, ch. lxv.

[15] Kavanaugh, Kieran and Rodriguez, Otilio (tr.). *The Collected Works of St. John of the Cross*, (Washington, D.C.: ICS Publications), 1964, p. 152.

[16] Kodloubovsky, E. and Palmer, G.E.H., *op. cit.* p. 235.

Chapter Seven: Development of Christian Meditation in Light of Yoga

[1] Epistle ad Diognetum cap. 5-6 in Pierre Pourrat *Christian Spirituality* (Westminster, MD: Newman Press), 1953, p. 37.

[2] Athanasius, Archbishop of Alexandria. "The Life of Saint Anthony" in *Stories of the Holy Fathers* translated by Ernest A. Wallis Budge (London: Oxford University Press), p. 10, 24.

[3] *Ibid.* p. lxix.

[4] Palladius "The Paradise" in Budge, *op. cit.*, p 193-194.

[5] John Meyendorff, *St. Gregory Palamas and Orthodox Spirituality* (New York: St. Vladimir Seminary Press), 1974, p. 36-38.

[6] Palladius, *op. cit.*, p. 193-194.

[7] St. Nikodimos and St. Makarios, *The Philokalia*, Vol. 1, Translated by G.E. H. Palmer, Phillip Sherrard, and Kallistos Ware (London: Faber & Faber), 1979, p. 60.

[8] *Ibid.*, p. 64.

[9] *Ibid.*, p. 65.

[10] *Ibid.*, p. 68.

11 Meyendorff, *op. cit.*, p. 24.

12 Igumen Chariton. *The Art of Prayer* trans. by E. Kadloubovsky (London: Faber & Faber), 1966, p. 77.

13 Pourrat, *op. cit.*, p. 241.

14 Dionysius the Areopagite. *The Mystical Theology* trans. C. E. Rolt (London: S. P. C. K.), 1971, p. 191.

15 Richard of St. Victor. *De Exterminatione Mali*, pt, 3, ch. 18.

16 Edmund Colledge. *The Medieval Mystics of England*, (New York: Sheed & Ward), 1962, p. 137-39.

17 Julian of Norwich. *Showings* trans Edmund Colledge and James Walsh (New York: Paulist Press), 1978, p. 265.

18 Catherine of Sienna. *Vita e Dottrina*, cap. 18 in Evelyn Underhill, Mysticism (New York: Dutton), 1961, p. 441.

19 *The Book of Privy Counseling*. ed. William Johnson (New York: Image Books), 1973, p. 156-57.

20 Pourrat, *op. cit.*, p. 23.

21 Ignatius of Loyola. *The Spiritual Exercises* trans. by Anthony Mattola (New York: Image Books) 1964.

22 Adolphe Tanquerey. *The Spiritual Life* trans by H. Branderis (Boston: Benziger Brother), 1930, p. 32.

23 Antonio Royo and Jordan Aumann. *The Theology of Christian Perfection* (Dubuque, IA: The Priory Press), 1962, p. 514.

24 *Ibid.*, p. 529.

25 *Ibid.*, p. 532-33.

26 Patanjali. *Yoga Sutras* trans. I. K. Taimni (Wheaton, IL: Theosophical Publishing House), 1975, section 3.2, p. 278.

27 *Theologia Germanica* trans. by Susanna Winkworth (London: Stuart and Watkins), 1966, p. 103.

28 Saint Athanasius. *The Incarnation of the Word Against the Nestorians* 1:108.

29 Meister Eckhart. *Sermon 99* in Underhill, op. cit, p. 420.

30 *De Quatuor Gradibus Violentae Charitatis in Patrologia Latina* (Paris) 1844-55, vol. 196.

31 Ruysbroeck. *De Calculo* in Underhill, *op. cit.*, p. 312-313.

32 Evelyn Underhill. *Practical Mysticism* (New York: Dutton), 1943, p. 3.

CHAPTER EIGHT: THE MEANING OF REVELATION

1 Hollander, R. *Allegory in Dante's Commedia* (Princeton: Princeton University Press), 1969. p. 23+.

CHAPTER ELEVEN: MIRACLES, SIDDHIS AND SCIENCE

1 Luther, Martin. "Sermons on the Gospel of Saint John" in *Luther's Works* edited by Jaroslav Pelikan (St. Louis: Concordia Publishers), 1955, ch. 14ff (24.367).

2 Calvin, John. *Institute of the Christian Religion* trans. by H. Beveridge (Grand Rapids, MI: Eerdmans), 1953, IV. 18, 2:636.

[3] Barth, Karl. *Church Dogmatics* edited and translated by G. W. Bromiley, T. F. Torrance, and others. (Edinburgh: T and T Clark), 1936-69.

[4] Bultmann, Rudolph. *Jesus Christ and Mythology* (New York: C. Scribner's Sons), 1958, p. 15.

[5] Bultmann, Rudolph, et al. *Kerygma and Myth* edited by H. Bartsch, revised edition of translation by R. H. Fuller (New York: Harper & Row), 1961, p. 4-5.

[6] St. Augustine. *City of God*, p. xxii.

[7] *Yoga Sutras of Patanjali*, I. 2, 5.

[8] *Ibid.*, II. 21.

[9] *Ibid.*, I. 24.

[10] The third pada of *The Yoga Sutras* outlines the range of control over the material realm available to the practitioner.

[11] *The Yoga Sutras of Patanjali* III. 45.

[12] Banerjee, S. *A Mystic Sage, Ma Anandamayi* (Calcutta: S. Banerjee), 1973, p. 82.

[13] Ram Dass. *Miracle of Love: Stories About Neem Karoli Baba* (New York: Dutton), 1979, p. 47; 285.

[14] Swami Rama. *Living with the Himalayan Masters* (Honesdale, PA: Himalayan Publishers), 1978, p. 400-01.

[15] See also the following works for a discussion of this concept: Charles Bates in *Ransoming the Mind* (St. Paul, MN: Yes International); Barbara Brown in *New Mind, New Body* (New York: Harper & Row); Fritz Capra in *The Tao of Physics* (New York: Bantam); and Elmer and Alyce Green in *Beyond Biofeedback* (New York: Delta).

CHAPTER TWELVE: CHRISTIAN GNOSTICISM AND YOGA

[1] James Robinson, ed., *The Nag Hammadi Library* (hereafter referred to as NHL), The Gospel of Truth, 13, 22, 1 (New York: Harper & Row), 1981.

[2] The Gospel of Philip, II, 3, 75 NHL, p. 147.

[3] *Mundaka Upanishad* II, 2, 10-11.

[4] The Gospel of Philip, II, 3, 84, NHL.

[5] Apocalypse of James, V, 3, 31, 15-26, NHL.

[6] Second Word of Seth, VII, 2, 55, 9-56, NHL.

[7] Revelation of Peter, VII, 3, 81, 3, NHL.

[8] Pagels, Elaine. *The Gnostic Gospels* (New York: Vintage Books, Random House), 1981, p. 62.

[9] Dialogue of the Savior, III, 5, 132, NHL.

[10] Testimony of Truth, IX, 3, 44, NHL.

[11] The Teachings of Silvanus, VII, 4, 86, NHL.

[12] The Gospel of Thomas, II, 2, 32, NHL.

INDEX

ABOUT THE AUTHOR

Justin O'Brien is a renaissance man: a philosopher, theologian, naturalist, wellness expert, yoga practitioner, and consultant in lifestyle management.

A pioneer in the exploration of consciousness, he is known nationally and internationally for his programs in spiritual development, wellness and aging, and leadership. His insights translate across East and West, self-care skills and scholarship, business and human development, organizational well-being and personal spiritual growth.

A consultant for world conferences on the future of humanity in Tokyo, Katmandu, and New Delhi, Dr. O'Brien is a gifted speaker and presenter. A well known scholar, he is former Professor of Theology at Loyola University Chicago, lecturer at the New School for Social Research in New York City, and Senior Research Fellow in Holistic Medicine at the University of London. He served as Director of Education at the Marylebone Health Centre, England, as well as faculty and Director of Education at the Himalayan International Institute of Yoga Science and Philosophy of the USA. He is currently principal of Justin O'Brien Associates: Consultants in Lifestyle Management, Professor of Philosophy at St. Mary's University Graduate School, and faculty at the University of St. Thomas and the Alpha Institute, all in Minneapolis/St. Paul.

His global travels and research throughout the world have enabled him to synthesize Western and Eastern concepts into a holistic framework for evolving human nature and its behavioral possibilities to higher levels of performance.

O'Brien holds a doctoral degree in the philosophy of consciousness and a doctorandus degree in theology from Nijmegen University, the Netherlands; masters degrees in philosophy and religious studies from Marquette University and St. Albert's College in Oakland, California; and undergraduate degrees in the classics and philosophy from the University of Notre Dame. He is a recognized scholar of Eastern philosophy and psychology and also a certified Ericksonian hypnotherapist from the American Hypnosis Training Academy.

Dr. O'Brien has authored *A Meeting of Mystic Paths, The Wellness Tree, Mirrors for Men, Christianity and Yoga, Running and Breathing,* and is contributing author to *Western Spirituality, The Spiral Path, Spirituality for the Religious Educator,* and *Meditation in Christianity.*